From the Streets to Corporate America: The Power of Mindset & Method

Corner to Cubicle

AMERVIS LÓPEZ COBB

Foreword by Adriana Rosales, CEO Adriana & Company™ LLC
Certified John Maxwell Speaker & Author of "Corporate Code"

FOR BULK PURCHASES AND KEYNOTE SPEAKING

Contact Amervis & Associates at

www.amervis.com

Copyright © 2019 by Amervis López Cobb, MBA, PMP®

You have permission to post, email, print and pass this book along for free to anyone you like, as long as you make no format or content changes. You are encouraged to quote passages and show clips in a review. However, the publisher prohibits binding and selling it, in whole or in part, for commercial gain. Also, the author reserves full control over any movie rights. Being the diligent goal-setter that she is, her vision of the future as it relates to the contents contained within this book consists of a collaborative effort with a legendary filmmaker who is known for his in-your-face approach to similar controversial subject matter. She envisions the role of her mother being portrayed by a multi-talented actress who helped launch a wave of female rappers by redefining a traditionally male genre before she set it off as a successful actress in her own right.

First Edition Release August 8, 2019
United States of America
Edited November 25, 2020

Paperback ISBN-13: 978-1-7339827-0-2
eBook ISBN-13: 978-1-7339827-1-9

CONTENTS

FOREWORD

It is a great honor to write the foreword for Amervis López Cobb for many reasons. One, because I believe every story must be shared and two, because every story can change the life of another for the better. Throughout my many years of speaking internationally, writing, and mentoring, I have come across impactful stories and stories that remain in my heart forever. However, I must say, Amervis' story is one that shook me to the core and reminded me that we have much work to do in our inner cities as it pertains to equal opportunity for all, life, liberty, and the right to pursue happiness.

When I was first given the advance copy for review, it was the beginning of a journey with an incredible writer and storyteller. Amervis' witty humor, realism, and resilience through tragedy is the key to her success both in life and in writing. They say that writing is never about the story itself but about the intensity of the story. This book is intense and keeps you on the edge of your seat. You will be changed forever, and that is what every great book does. It allows you to see the world from a different place, and in return, the book blesses you with a different perspective. Amervis does this masterfully and gracefully with every sentence full of truth, joy, heartbreak, and adventure. Her own story has shaped her, and that is the reason for her strong will and determination.

She has broken glass ceilings, healed race divisions, and gives us a taste of what it truly means to thrive against all the odds. Her story of valor, optimism, and ingenious strategic methods will revolutionize the way we view each other, our communities, our work and ultimately the world. It gives us a glimpse of what American children go through in inner cities. Amervis shows us what it takes to come out winning and thriving.

May you be as blessed by Amervis' story as I was. I'll be waiting with anticipation for her next book.

Adriana Rosales

Adriana Rosales, CEO Adriana & Company™ LLC
Certified John Maxwell Speaker & Author of "Corporate Code"

DEDICATION

My children and soul family, I wrote this book for you!

If you can derive value in stories told to inform and inspire you to new heights or transformational perspectives, this book is dedicated to you.

I am thrilled it is in your hands or on your electronic device. It is no coincidence. Blood is not the only thing binding us. In the deepest of ways, we are all connected to the positive power source fueling the entire universe with the love we must learn to show ourselves and others. I also dedicate this book to the following:

- Philadelphia, PA, where my journey in this world began. The city where I first reached one of many crossroads, decided what kind of woman I would become and learned to rise stronger.

- My grandmother, Catalina Torres, for being a woman of value with the character to set us in the right direction. She moved me toward action and instilled discipline to follow through.

- My mother, Ana López, who taught me to defend myself and fight when the alternative is to die. A strong-willed woman who did the best she could with what she had and embraced music to cope and connect to the inner recesses of her soul.

- My soul sister Loilda Ann Diaz, who gave me shelter beyond the structure of her home. A dear friend who was placed in my life to remind me, tall or small, God loves us all.

- My children Orlando, Zeana and Anabella, my most precious blessings, gifted to me when I needed each of them the most. They filled and fill my heart with happiness, just like my handsome grandsons Nando and Leo (who is on his way). These beautiful souls continuously teach me the meaning of love and inspire me to keep loving, learning and growing.

APPRECIATION

Foremost, I would like to express my appreciation to my husband, Philip Cobb, for his love and patience throughout the process of my finishing this book. I could not have imagined a better partner to join the family I created and have another child with after finding each other in Vegas. Ours is a story I am looking forward to sharing when the time is right. I am grateful God orchestrated our meeting. I had no idea when I sarcastically responded to his first words to me that behind his welcoming smile, he really did have game.

I also want to sincerely thank everyone God has blessed me with who I've known in one or more phase of my life; those who helped me optimize resources to maximize my potential, engaged in positive talk therapy and offered insightful, supportive commentary as I shared my writing goals.

I am especially grateful to and express my most profound appreciation for the individuals who prodded my expansion on my book publishing journey such as the following:

- Les Brown for his advice on July 6, 2019 and endorsement.
- Adriana Rosales for a heart-centered approach to coaching.
- Sharon Simmons and Martina Gordon for project feedback.
- Valerie Banks and Candace Schiessel for the status inquiries.
- Everyone who traveled across neighborhood, city, and state lines to attend my Philadelphia Pre-Release Book Talk, Reading, and Mixer events the weekend of June 22, 2019.
- My Master Your Masterpiece Mentor, Terri Liggins of *The Literary Front* for all she did and taught about writing.
- Magnificent 7's Dr. Jacqueline Sawyer and Sherma Felix as well as Mary Hawver and Allen Plunkett for detailed edits.
- Jodi Friedman and Velda Morris for the encouragement.
- Lindsay Parker for the back of the book cover photo assist.
- Christina Aldan for her inspiring authenticity and fierceness.

Chapter One
Brave or Broken

"When you keep searching for ways to change your situation for the better, you stand a chance of finding them. When you stop searching, assuming they can't be found, you guarantee they won't." ~ Angela Duckworth

I have lived in many worlds that have challenged my mindset and driven me to adopt proven methods to success in one way or another all my life. I learned hard lessons before reaching adulthood and continued to do so in my 40s.

At an early age, it was clear, to survive and thrive meant first becoming familiar with and cultivating a growth mindset, which had more to do with attitude and action, than fast talk and limited movement.

Throughout my journey, it has become more apparent than ever; possessing a mindset focused on growth is the first ingredient in any recipe for success. The most valuable insight I gained from my professional journey is that without the right mindset, methods, and perseverance; progress might come to a standstill or be slower than necessary.

The operative word here is perseverance. According to Merriam Webster's dictionary, it means "continued effort to do or achieve something despite difficulties, failure, or opposition."

I say this with the understanding that most of us are aware of the need to be determined if we want to overcome obstacles or take advantage of opportunities to level up. However, those of us who get this also know determination alone is not enough to successfully maneuver the complexity of certain systems in life.

In many cases, females and people of diverse backgrounds, have to work even harder when things get hard to look deeply within, to believe. To believe we have what it takes to break through structures created to disenfranchise the least among us.

There will be times when some of us will encounter challenging situations that will force us to answer the question, "Am I going to entertain thoughts and the belief that I am broken?" Or...

Will I be brave enough to own my past, present and future stories?

In the past, I often entertained the idea of being broken. I now know it is a false statement. Neither the cut-throat cultures of the North Philadelphia Badlands nor the ones of Corporate America were able to break me, though both could have.

To get from point A to point B, I had to continuously open my mind to new possibilities and seek new methods to rise stronger. It is how I survived toxic environments, maintained my sanity, and continuously reinvented myself. Consistently striving to bulk up my knowledge and skillset helped me make strides professionally and kept me competitive in the job market.

After two decades in various management and leadership positions with multiple organizations, I had finally achieved a dream of becoming an Information Technology Vice President (VP). Just over a year and a half into this particular organizational culture, I found myself at a career crossroad. The story of how I became a VP and what was done in an attempt to break my spirit is worthy of becoming a Lifetime movie script or an ABC 20/20 television show episode.

If I expended enough energy on it, an entire book could be filled with the events which occurred during those crucial months of learning. Instead, I decided to focus on healing. I started by taking books off my bookshelf and re-reading highlights I made in the following:

- Rising Strong, by Brené Brown
- Mindset: The New Psychology of Success, by Carol S. Dweck
- Grit: The Power of Passion and Perseverance, by Angela Duckworth

I revisited the famous words of a dynamic man who was internationally known to rock his microphone. One of his most referred to quotes kept making its way into the forefront of my mind: *"Shoot for the moon. Even if you miss, you'll land among the stars."*

The world's most renowned motivational speaker, Les Brown, gave me cause to pause and revisit those words I had heard in the past. Words I repeated myself when speaking to women in leadership groups on the topic of career elevation.

I analyzed these thirteen words over and over with the idea of taking risks and the end result being better than I was before I started, even if I did not get what I initially targeted. It made a lot of sense and sounded like the start of a smart plan.

Les' words, coupled with others I was exposing myself to, made me give serious thought to seeking new ways to live a more purpose-driven life. As a result, I reached down into the grave, grabbed one of my dreams and began the process of resurrecting it.

Simultaneously, I updated my resume and made an effort to secure work. I aligned my skills, knowledge and abilities, but more importantly, my values, and what I brought to the table.

In my youth, as well as in three decades of corporate life, I witnessed a common misconception about success coming to those with natural-born talent or relationships based on networking efforts alone. While both are vital ingredients for sustainability, it works best for some of us when talent and networking are mixed with Mindset and Method (MM).

In my experience, it was only when I sought and applied new knowledge through planning and execution that I was able to understand the full value of the MM factor. It served me well nearly thirty years ago and continues to today. It stands for:

Mindset + Method = Success

The key word here is success. According to Merriam Webster's dictionary, it means the degree or measure of succeeding: favorable or desired outcome.

In my mind, success had become relative. It was comparable to the goals one sets for himself. To me—and perhaps to most people who strive for it—success almost always meant freedom.

In this memoir, you will encounter the story of a young girl from a diverse background — one who hears the whispers of an inside

4

voice. A voice that repeatedly prompts her to shoot for the moon.

You will get to know a youngster who starts as a vulnerable female character, encounters many challenges, and begins to transform and grow, setting the foundation for goal achievement.

I invite you on a journey with a child who recognizes and listens to the near-deafening sound of a roar compelling her to take action to own her past, present, and future story.

What lies in the pages ahead is the exploration of the world as seen through her eyes.

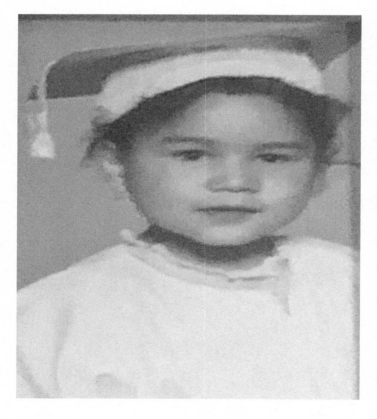

You will encounter examples of mindsets and methods she

deployed to maneuver through the badlands of life. You will get to know a young girl who confronts one insurmountable obstacle after another within a Philadelphia cut-throat culture before finally creating a strategy to break free from a generational cycle of poverty.

Chapter Two
Breaking Point

"Hate, it has caused a lot of problems in the world but has not solved one yet." ~ Maya Angelou

When I was a child, my mother was a juvenile who was not capable of taking care of herself, much less her children. As she explored her adulthood, which included me, my adolescence and teen years, it was apparent Ana wanted to be free from the burdens of childcare.

Her behavior fueled my desire to move out of the squatter house she unlawfully occupied after her last eviction. While my childhood was painful and the circumstances worse than ever, I clung to thoughts of hope in the face of what felt like endless adversity. I wondered how people who descended from impoverished situations similar to my own coped with being abused and treated like an afterthought when it came to the guardianship of adults who were preoccupied with their addictions.

Disheartened by a lack of love and too many fate-altering incidents that only served to perpetuate a generational cycle of poverty, I felt an immense undertaking to seize any overarching and sustainable control over my life. Never was this clearer to me than on an ill-fated Philly afternoon as I stepped off the 47 onto the concrete sidewalk on the corner of the bus stop at 6th and Tioga Streets.

The day will forever stand out in my mind because I was shocked by what I heard coming out of my mother's mouth. As I crossed the street, heading east toward Randolph Street, I hadn't the slightest clue about what awaited me inside the walls of that three-story brick row home. I walked up to the drab porch and made my way through the run-down front door.

I stepped over some empty beer bottles in the living room and within seconds, discovered my mother hunkered down, creatively using a hollow Coke can as a hollowed means of transmission for burning crack on one end while inhaling on the other. I couldn't believe she possessed the ingenuity to turn a cylindrical metal container meant to hold soda into a makeshift pipe. Smoke permeated throughout the air in that dilapidated house devoid of light and filled with scattered crack vials.

Once again, I found myself wondering why my mother could not just stop doing drugs and get some professional help. Irritated by my presence at the most inopportune moment, she replied with an appeal of her own, conveyed with nothing but cruelty in her voice. At the end of our interaction, I was crystal clear she wanted me to fast-track getting shacked up already.

I cannot recall her exact words. I will, however, always recall how she made me feel before I was encouraged to move out of the house on the 3500 block of Randolph street. I thought about how cold-hearted she was toward her fifteen-year-old virgin daughter.

Even in the midst of numerous roadblocks, I had always gotten myself to school on my own and forced thoughts of failure out of my mind daily. Now I had to deal with my mother demanding I do whatever it took to convince my seventeen-year-old boyfriend to let me move in with him and his parents. All so she could get high without the risk of me interrupting her as she engaged in her favorite pastime activity.

I wondered if perhaps it was possible that subconsciously, my mother didn't want me to catch her in the middle of doing something even worse, like heroin. I would later discover heroin was on her intoxication rotation menu; depending on what she could get her hands on.

After the death of my grandmother, I never grieved the unseen losses experienced by most offspring of an addict; such as the forfeiture of affection, a missing-in-action custodian, and the complete opposite of an untroubled happy childhood. Despite the

9

risks and consequences, my mother remained on the path of self-destruction, fueled by compulsive substance abuse day in and day out.

On this dismal late afternoon, I was more miserable than ever. I felt powerless. There was no point in crying out for help. There was no one around to help me keep what little was left of my fire lit or stoke it before it went completely dark.

I retreated quietly with palpitations mounting inside my chest. As I made my way out of the dining room, I turned left, looked at the chipped wood in the stairway before me, and carried my psychic burden up each step. I made another left at the top of the stairs and nearly dragged myself into the room I occupied in the middle of the house.

I had no idea what I was going to do. I couldn't figure out how to help my mother see that what she was doing could have an irreparable effect on our relationships and our collective well-being.

I knew there was a real risk of my mother losing her life sooner than what any of us could have ever imagined. Didn't she know that heart disease ran in our family? She didn't seem aware or care that an increasing addiction to cocaine could bring on a heart attack at any age much faster.

The minuscule hope I had been hanging on to nearly vanished. My insides ached from the feeling of not having any real control over the situation. All I could feel was a tightening in my upper body. I was emotionally crushed and on the brink of a complete breakdown. Feeling defeated, I plopped face down onto the stained mattress with my face purposefully positioned over an uncovered pillow. I did my best to conceal the sounds of my muffled uncontrollable wailing.

I thought to myself, *"Daayyum[1], I can't believe she just dissed[2] me like that; everything in this jawn[3] is not aight[4]. She already sold all da[5] stuff Mami left us when she died and was hustling food stamps to get faded[6]. Now she's gonna[7] be stealing from other people's cribs[8] so she could cop[9] drugs, causing me to be more assed out[10] than ever. She can't keep this on the down low[11] long. Soon enough, she'll be out on the streets with even less shame, drawlin[12] and acting like a real fiend for da rock! My moms[13] was gonna[14] get bum rushed[15] or chin checked[16] if she didn't chill[17]. God forbid what she was doing led her to get toe-tagged[18].*

When I was asked, "what's crack-a-lack-in?"[19] the first thing that came to my mind would be my mom is cracking[20]..."

I thought it but could never say it. I figured I would start bugging out[21] as a distraction. Not only had my mother chosen her new drug of choice over me, she wanted me gone so she could light her processed cocaine transformed into a crystal rock in peace without

---

1 Damn
2 Dismissed or not good
3 Person (usually a woman), Place or Thing – in this context, it is a place (house)
4 Contraction of all right
5 The
6 High, stoned, drunk
7 Going to
8 House, residence
9 Get a hold of
10 Out of luck, screwed
11 Discreet, kept private
12 Acting out of character, doing something others do not approve of
13 Mother
14 Going to
15 Attacked
16 Jab to the mandible
17 Relax
18 Deceased person in a morgue
19 Happening
20 Popping sounds when crack is heated
21 Freaking out

having to hear the outcry against her actions or lack thereof. Once I managed to swallow the lump in my throat, numbness set in. All I could focus on was my desperation and not being smart enough to make it stop.

My grandmother ignited the fire in me regularly. When she disappeared from physical existence and my fire nearly died out, every once in a while, a genuinely caring teacher who I will always remember, Ms. Dorothy Page, shook the logs around and blew lightly to provide much-needed spurts of oxygen. The type of quick breaths she gave me prodded me into expansion and provided the push I needed throughout that period to continuously seek part-time work while riding and remaining on the learning and education train. Going to school also provided a system of rules, which I made reasonable efforts to follow. Now my home life was affecting my ability to concentrate at school or do homework after.

As a youth coming of age in the late 1980s, the commercial, "This is your brain on drugs. Any questions?" was memorable. I certainly did not want to fathom the thought of my brain being likened to a fried egg. This large-scale US anti-narcotics campaign and televised public service announcement (PSA) had no impact on my household and barely any on my community at large.

Then there was a stranger in the back of my head whose voice jumped at every chance to remind me I didn't fit in where I was and no one at Central would ever accept me into their circle. Whenever I listened to it, if I had a smile, it would turn upside down. It made ongoing attempts to convince me I would never be smart enough.

Chapter Three
Broken Spirit

"Stress is the trash of modern life--we all generate it, but if you don't dispose of it properly, it will pile up and overtake your life." ~
Danzae Pace

The following day, I didn't go to school. I could barely get out of bed. When I finally mustered up the strength to pull myself up, I brushed my teeth, threw a hat on and headed east. I walked south over the mini bridge on 5th street toward my best friend Wil's crib[22] on the 2800 block of North Hope Street. Less than thirty minutes later, I knocked on a beat-up-looking door similar to the one I had departed from on Randolph street. This door was next to the house on the corner of Cambria Street. I was quietly ushered inside.

As her pale, porcelain skin and dark brown mullet[23] greeted me with a chin-up, she asked, "You straight?[24] " I replied, "I will be when we get some cheeba[25] up in here." She said, "Ima[26] go get a nick[27], just need you to watch the kids." She hollered up the stairs,"Youse[28]"okay?" Before waiting to hear a response, she made her way upstairs.

---

22 House
23 Hairstyle cut short at the front and sides, but left long at the back
24 Good, okay or cool
25 Cannabis, marijuana of choice
26 I'm going to
27 Five-dollar baggie of marijuana
28 Plural for you

I was left in front of the sink with some potatoes on a cutting board next to it. After rinsing them off and dicing them, I placed them into a pot of water. I cut an onion in half and started crying. I lit a match using the burner on the stove in front of me before immediately blowing it out to stop the cut-up onion from making my eyes water.

I opened up a package of cubed beef, rinsed it off under the sink with water and placed the meat in the now boiling water. I added some Goya Adobo seasoning and a pack of Sazon seasoning and mixed the beef around.

I heard her yell on the way out, "I know you stressed but don't bogart[29] the ganja[30] when I get back!"

As soon as I heard the front door close behind her, a couple of tears I was holding back made their way out. This time, I wasn't crying because I was cutting another onion; I was tearing up because I couldn't control my angst anymore.

In the middle of that ill-fated attempt to cook Spanish style stew in the house with a handful of loud and hungry children, I bawled a little and quickly sucked my tears back in when I thought I heard one of them coming down the stairs.

Although I was physically present and expressed a desire to feed the children a meal they could tolerate going into their bellies, my mind was elsewhere and not really engaged in the present moment at what I was doing.

False alarm. I refocused on my concoction, tasted it, and added some more Adobo seasoning before taste testing it again. Another packet of Sazon soon followed. It gave the stew some much-needed

---

29 Selfishly appropriate
30 Marijuana

flavor, but it still wasn't thick enough and was missing another essential ingredient. I couldn't put my finger on it, but I knew adding something else would make it almost edible. I looked inside the cabinets, and there wasn't much in there to work with to put into the stew.

Wil lived in a small two-bedroom row home with her mother, Pat; her two sisters when they managed to make it home and all of their children. To say it was a full house was an understatement as I rattled off their names, "Luis, Liza, Jose, Eric, and Steven, dinner should be ready in about an hour." When Wil had Steven a couple of years earlier, she didn't go back to school. Instead, she dropped out to help her mother take care of all her grandchildren.

I stared almost blindly into the pot of boiling beef, repeatedly stirring it until I felt a tap on my shoulder. Wil found me where she left me, in her tiny kitchen, going through the motions, while immobilized by the vastness of my life-changing predicament. I was startled, which prompted me to turn the flame down low and place the stirring spoon next to the stove.

I followed Wil as she made her way toward the front of the house. She stopped short of the door and plopped onto the plastic-covered couch, reached for my hand, and gently pulled me toward her until I found myself firmly seated on the sofa. She put her arm around my shoulder and handed me a rolled-up ready to smoke marijuana blunt. She smiled and said what we said to each other almost every time we hung out, "Light up!"

I smirked and slowly moved the lighter close to my face, my hands shaking from the freezing winter weather that made its way inside the house through the gaps in the old windows and doors. I pressed my lips around the blunt, inhaled, and let out a few coughs within the first few seconds. She laughed and said, "Okay now, puff, puff, pass."

And there we were, the two of us—she was seventeen, I was fifteen—puffing on a marijuana blunt as a way to manage our stress. We coped as best we could and made a weak attempt to identify strategies to get from point A to point B. Our vision for the future most definitely consisted of an alternate reality in a better space and a much better place than the one we had been experiencing.

I caught her up on what happened the day before on Randolph Street. I shared how, instead of working on igniting my fire or helping me stabilize it and prevent it from going out, watching my mother hold a lighter to a Coke can felt like she was drowning my dreams by pouring water over the fire inside my belly. It was heart-wrenching. Trying to figure out what to do or how to do it was a monumental undertaking given the way I was feeling.

I told Wil that even though I anguished over this, I was livid that my mother made no attempt to hide her evolving lifestyle. A lifestyle which now consisted of drinking forty ounces of beer, sniffing glue, smoking pot, snorting cocaine, and now shamelessly smoking crack right in front of her own daughter.

Recounting the Coke can incident, and the cumulative effect of all the drama affected my pulse. I felt like exploding! Wil responded to the look on my face, "That's messed up; you got enough book smarts to make it out." To which I replied, "It isn't enough."

It seemed impossible to get out of this turmoil without engaging in compromising behavior, willingly or unwillingly. We talked about growing up around addicts being the norm for people like us.

I tried to joke about just wanting to live in a safe and stable home with enough food, hot water, and non-kerosene heat, but it wasn't funny. Evidence of my mother's life being unmanageable surfaced well before I was born.

Focusing on anything was a bit of challenge as was getting to school at all. When I did go, it was with limited sleep or clean clothes that didn't smell weird. Some days it was exhausting to make a mad dash up and down the stairs with pots of boiling water trying to quickly wash up before the bathtub water turned cold again.

I despised the children in school who teased me about my clothes not being washed in Tide. Sometimes, I soaked my clothes in the sink with dishwashing liquid and rinsed them before hanging to dry. Seeing my mother use a can to smoke crack was the straw that damn near broke my camel-ass back.

It was only a few short months earlier that my older cousin went to some guy's house, and as usual, I was told to go with her. When it started to get late, I begged her to leave. It wasn't too long before she took me to a bar. I didn't want to get in trouble again. I kept telling my cousin we had to go but she would not listen to me.

When the lyrics to the song, *Nightmares* by Dana Dane, started playing, in walked my aunt to firmly escort us out of there. By the time we got back to my aunt's house, there was a belt waiting for us with both our names on it. Not only did I get whipped, but I was also advised to pack up what little belongings I had and ordered into my aunt's car.

I couldn't believe my cousin's unwillingness to listen to me jeopardized my living situation, and I would end up paying the penalty in more ways than one. I was kicked out, and it had nothing to do with a shortcoming or deficiency on my part.

Since I was a minor without any family members who were willing or able to take me in, I wondered how long it would be before Child Protective Services, or the Department of Human Services showed up to shepherd me into the system.

I spent a lot of time wondering why I was born into poverty.

Why was my mother on drugs?

Why didn't anyone want me?

What I didn't know at the time and what would take me decades to realize is **sometimes we don't get what we want because it is not in alignment with our soul.**

Chapter Four
Broken Badlands Born

"Study the past if you would define the future." ~ Confucius

A llow me to introduce myself. I arrived in this world on October 11, 1972, in a city occupied by nearly two million people that was part of a state prominent to the formation of American history; within a country that had just gone through the Watergate scandal involving Republican President Richard M. Nixon. He had been elected to a second term less than a month after I was born.

At the time, the New York Times would refer to the city as the Graffiti Capital of the World, and Time Magazine estimated there were about 10,000 street artists. The Declaration of Independence, the United States Constitution, and I were all born in the same place, Philadelphia; a place in the United States made up of over thirty neighborhoods, each with their distinctive sub-cultures.

I first showed my face to this world inside the walls of Saint Mary's Hospital, located at 1601 East Palmer Street in the vicinity of East Girard Avenue. The area was one of many urban and densely populated neighborhoods within the *City of Brotherly Love*.

As a youth, I would venture out on foot and via Southeast Pennsylvania's Public Transportation Authority (SEPTA) and explore some of the city's best neighborhoods like Mount Airy, Center City's Rittenhouse Square, and Old City's Society Hill. But I would be raised in a section of the city made up of an arid territory collectively known as the Badlands.

While in the hospital, my mother filled out paperwork that all public institutions from that time on would use to refer to me as Amervis López. I am not sure why my mother, Ana, decided against writing my father's last name, Saez, next to mine on my birth certificate, as the practice of doing so was common in Puerto Rican culture. I can only assume she was conflicted because, in addition to denying me my father's namesake, she would often cast me aside from the day I was born. It would have been ideal if my mother had positively responded to hearing the lyrics "*I Can See Clearly Now*" by Johnny Nash, which was popular around the time I was born.

She never had a crisis of conscience after giving birth to me. Neither her loving feelings for my father nor the arrival of her two children, one of whom was born nearly three years earlier, brought her any sustainable clarity of mind or maternal instincts. By the time I was born, my mother had been a middle school drop out for almost five years, and she had no intention of ever making her way back to school.

Her chosen occupation was similar to that of a gypsy or nomad, who sought roofs filled with warmth, love, and acceptance. As a teenager, she wandered from place to place and eventually began an on-again-off-again love affair with my father. His name was Manuel, and he was a factory worker who moved from his birthplace in Puerto Rico to Philly a few years earlier before they met. Theirs was a roller-coaster relationship in the early to mid-seventies.

After leaving the hospital, my mother's eldest sister, Santa, took me in. She lived on the 2nd and 3rd floors atop a three-story low-income row home apartment building on North Marshall Street; near the corner of Columbia Street later renamed Cecil B Moore.

There were a few Puerto Ricans in this North Philadelphia neighborhood, but the majority of the population was African American. This part of the city, like too many others, was typical of an urban ghetto populated primarily by poor people living in run-down homes with limited greenery on any horizon. Most of the exterior walls around the neighborhood displayed street art created by real, fake, and aspiring gang members that would tag names to represent their block or an entire territory.

My mother, Ana López Torres was the daughter of Lorenzo López and Catalina Torres. She was born on August 10, 1955 in Ponce, Puerto Rico, a mere eighteen days before the United States civil rights movement exploded following the murder of Emmett Till, a 14-year-old African American boy falsely accused of whistling at a white woman.

My maternal grandfather, Lorenzo López, looked like he could pass for Emmett's father. My grandfather was what I would consider Afro-Rican because he was a darker-skinned Boricua born and raised in Puerto Rico. If he never opened his mouth for one to hear his native tongue, he'd be mistaken in the States for being 100% African American. His features consisted of a darker-than-caramel brown complexion, coarse gray hair, and relatively full nose.

I didn't know anything else about my mother's lineage beyond her grandparents and the fact that Lorenzo's mother was named Felicitas López. My parents and my mother's family left Puerto Rico in route to Philadelphia as soon as they became aware of the industrial jobs still driving the local economy. They moved close to accessible, low-cost housing. My aunt Santa, uncle Edwin, and my father Manuel all landed manufacturing jobs, while others like my grandmother, remaining aunts, and mother relied on various means of assistance.

It is my understanding that I wasn't with my aunt Santa long before she dropped me off to live with my maternal grandmother in another low-income apartment within a similar North Philadelphia neighborhood called Hartranft. She lived up the block from the corner of Germantown Avenue and Dauphin Streets in an area made up of a slightly higher concentration of Puerto Ricans. It was still predominantly occupied by African Americans.

My brother was already living with my grandmother and no one in my family could ever explain why I wasn't taken there from the day I was born. My mother would visit periodically but she rarely seemed happy when she stepped foot inside my grandmother's apartment. My brother and I lived with my grandmother because my mother was considered by some to be the primary antagonistic force in the family. Too wild to raise her children; my mother had no concerns with grandmother taking over the hands-on child-rearing responsibilities.

When family visited, you could hear them as they reached the second floor of our apartment. The top step led up and into the living room, bathroom, kitchen, bedroom on the second floor, and two small bedrooms were on the third floor. The entranceway from the kitchen led to stairs to the third-floor bedrooms and curtain beads in the doorway within a tiny corridor. On the other side of the beaded door, in the opposite direction of the kitchen, was the living room, which consisted of the most abundant space in the apartment with two windows that faced the front of the house.

The living room walls had a velvet-textured, cream and paisley cranberry patterned wallpaper. My grandmother also had a matching cranberry-colored sofa set with gold accented coffee and end tables with glass tops. She had small elephant figures sitting atop of them facing the front entryway for good luck.

Then there was the sacred wood-like rocking chair made of a wicker seat and wicker backing. In our curiosity, it would serve us well to not destroy any parts of my grandmother's beaded entryway, the intriguing wallpaper, or any of her belongings, let alone be caught sitting in her wicker rocking chair.

I was not allowed into my grandmother's bedroom much; it was in the back of the apartment with the only entry point from the kitchen, which had two windows facing the abandoned lot where another house used to exist before it had been torn down. There was a gas station on the opposite side of our building that sandwiched in our apartment with the empty lot on the opposite side. The stairs leading to the third floor led into the first bedroom, which was extremely small and contained a twin bed against the wall.

Before reaching my bedroom, we passed spiritual items such as a Virgin Mary sculpture, Jesus' face imprinted on candles, and superstitious paraphernalia against walls adjacent to a small window facing the yard and kitchen rooftop. She was a devout Catholic; she prayed to "Papa Dios"[31].

She would also leave pennies soaking underwater near an Indian Chief Head. Beside it sat a burgundy carved statue of a Buddha with a big round belly and crossed legs.

The first bedroom upstairs led into the second bedroom where my brother and I slept with our beds close to the two front windows. My brother and I would fight often; sometimes, he would beat me up and sometimes I would sneak a punch in an offensive or defensive move. Mostly we wrestled until we were tired and out of breath. On occasion, we would lie down on our backs with our legs raised in the air and feet touching, simulating bicycle-circling motions until we were exhausted.

The landlord lived on the first floor. He was the oldest white man I had ever seen, except for those we watched on the television. He was a kind man who expressed interest in our household and would sometimes hand us grocery bags in more than cordial gestures toward my grandmother.

---

31 God, our Father

Some of my earliest memories of growing up were in the second and third floor of our three-story low-income apartment building on the northwest side of the 2300 block of North Germantown Avenue.

The apartment was only a street block away from St. Edward's Catholic Church located on the Northeast corner of North 8th Street and West York Street. It was a city block up the street from the Ile Ife Museum. Ile Ife was the first place I saw and touched African and African American art in the form of colorful textured paintings and striking sculptures from the spiritual heartland of the Yoruba in Nigeria. I learned in the Yoruba language Ile Ife meant House of Love, which it felt like whenever my brother and I visited the place on the corner of Dauphin Street and Germantown Avenue in the 1970s.

I was enrolled in daycare and kindergarten two blocks north from the Ile Ife museum. As soon as I arrived, I immediately made friends with most of the African American girls, and they wanted to do my hair. They would tell me they liked it, which I didn't understand because I thought my curls were unruly and tough to comb out when they got dry. The girls would ask me if they could braid it, an offer I happily accepted. A few times, they braided my hair like Stevie Wonder's shoulder-length style, with multiple individual braids all around my head secured by wooden beads and aluminum foil at the bottom of each twist. When it was complete, I swung my hair side to side.

If I didn't keep still when my grandmother was taking it apart along with the knots that developed in my hair, she would knock me over the head with a hard Avon brush before pulling it all back into a single ponytail or parting it in the middle. She'd make two ponytails, which was the style I preferred. I knew that was the direction she was headed in when she'd gather all my hair on one side and secure it with a ponytail holder before repeating the same steps on the other. She'd comb out the ends, wrap all the hair on that side around her finger, and then remove it from her finger to form one big bulky curl.

While still wet, she would repeat the same steps on the other side of my head, and slick down the curls that peeked out along my hairline by pressing the brush firmly against my scalp and pushing the hairs managing to get loose downward. When I arrived at school, tiny curls would pop out from the ponytails, and my two fat bulky curls would widen in comparison to what they looked like when they were wet.

Chapter Five
Broken Family

"The justifications of men who kill should always be heard with skepticism..." ~ Patrick Ness

D espite the love my parents felt for each other, I was born out of wedlock. My mother, Ana, also known as Anita at home and Billy Boy in the streets, had a butch-like appearance and demeanor.

My father and mother listened to all kinds of music. Some of the artists I heard growing up were KC and the Sunshine Band and Donna Summer. I could listen to songs like *"Love To Love You Baby"* and *"Isn't She Lovely"* by Stevie Wonder. I would imagine my father singing these songs to my mother.

Life in the hood was volatile, and so was their relationship. I imagined they went back and forth between the sentiments of songs like Three Degrees' *"When Will I See You Again,"* Barry White's *"Can't Get Enough of Your Love, Babe,"* and Rufus featuring Chaka Khan's *"You Got the Love"* to Roberta Flack's *"Killing Me Softly With His Song."*

Before I graduated from kindergarten and got to know him, I lost my father forever. I would never be able to take advantage of the opportunity to grow up and experience the father-daughter bond resulting from years of love exhibited by the only man who had ever shown genuine respect for my mother.

My father's last day in this world was in a place which would eventually become recognized by its residents and the press as the notorious Philadelphia Badlands. Being a child of Spanish ancestry living in financially constrained conditions in the Badlands meant there was a high probability I would encounter disappointment at some point in my childhood. Inevitably, most of us who grew up without fathers would be affected by psychological and physical circumstances leading to a multitude of frustrations.

Frustrations ran rampant almost daily in the air inhaled within those narrow streets of Philadelphia within the zip codes occupied by those of us living in poverty. It was the mid-seventies when my father was playing pool at a neighborhood bar with a fellow factory worker, my uncle Edwin. My father was on a winning streak.

After he won his last pool game, my uncle warned him they should leave the bar because angry pool-losing drunks in the inner city offered a high probability of being not-so-good sportsmen. As it was in my father's case, he wasn't playing against a man who could nobly accept defeat and take on what he learned throughout the game to improve his future posture.

Quite the contrary, on that ill-fated Philly night, the murderous loser returned to the bar later in the evening and gunned downed my father in plain sight. It was sometime around the Bicentennial Celebration of the United States in 1976 when my father ignored the warning that someone could be such a dreadfully sore loser.

He underestimated the man with whom he had more game. The man who would return with a firearm and take a life over the loss of a billiard game created to be fun-filled, not blood spilled. After my father's organs shut down, his funeral was planned to take place in Puerto Rico on the island where he had been born. An island I never had the opportunity to discover beyond a quick harbor passthrough before moving on to other Caribbean islands.

The song most appropriate for that season was *"Only the Good Die Young"* by Billy Joel. I'd listened to it while looking at the only picture I had of my father and me. He's holding me next to my mother. I am sandwiched between them, held up by his muscular arms. Because of my chubby cheeks and slightly slanted eyes when I was a baby, I was nicknamed China, pronounced "Cheena."

I only had this one picture of my father to stare at now and then, wondering if I looked like him and why I had to live life without his presence. For years, I attempted to peek into his soul by looking intensely into the expression on his face and his eyes.

I didn't know anything about my father's family on the island or anywhere else for that matter, except for the fact he had a brother everyone called Papo, who also moved to Philly when my father left Puerto Rico. I only remember meeting Papo twice when I was a child after my father passed away. He took me to the candy store across the street where we lived on Germantown Avenue. He bought me some Laffy Taffy Candy, probably an act of pity, feeling slightly sorry for me after my father died.

A few short years later, he gave my mother some money to purchase clothes for me. To my surprise, she actually used it for that very purpose. She bought me a couple of pairs of Chic Jeans at

Kmart. That whole act felt like a payoff and later it was confirmed as such. A payoff because not too long after I was rocking those jeans, I found out Papo got my mother's roommate pregnant and I never saw him again.

Years later, I found out my father had a daughter in Puerto Rico and one in Philly. Having never been to Puerto Rico, I haven't been able to confirm this as fact.

Regarding the sister in Philly, when I was about twenty and shopping with my mother at the Franklin Mills Mall in Northeast Philly, my mother said she recognized my sister's mother across the room in a Long John Silver's restaurant. She went over to make conversation because her teenage daughter resembled my father. However, after I asked the light-skinned young girl with long relatively straight soft hair if she wanted to exchange phone numbers, both she and her mother brushed us off in an air of elite Puerto Rican superiority.

I told my mother I was ready to go and gestured toward the parking garage. As I walked toward the car, I made up my mind there was no point in trying to push myself on anyone, even a blood relative, if they had no interest in connecting.

After my father died, my mother became intimate with women in her lesbian associations and social clubs. Some of my family members raised eyebrows when she showed up dressed in men clothing during her sporadic visits.

When the topic of my mother wearing men's clothing came up, I could hear in my grandmother's voice, the sound of disdain, even in her native Spanish tongue and broken English. The tone in my grandmother's voice would always get high after one of my mother's "girlfriends" called the house asking for "Billy Boy". Ana could be called Anita, but "Billy Boy" was unwelcomed.

I vividly recall my mother going all out with Bruce Lee Karate gear. She was thrilled to wear the black top and pants with her Chinese shoes. I was glad she was happy wearing these clothes because it made her feel good.

Like most Puerto Ricans living in Philly, there was usually a lot of screaming whenever and wherever two or more assembled. There was extra hollering in my grandmother's apartment when my mother came around, which never lasted long.

Once, a few weeks after my mother had moved out again, my grandmother gave her permission to pick me up for a sleepover.

While I was with my mother, she bought me some black ankle boots, a burgundy pullover sweater, gray denim pants, and a matching denim jacket. I was about five years old, and she slicked my hair straight back into a single ponytail to hold it all together. She had me hold the jacket over my shoulder and told me to smile like I was a badass while she took my picture standing on the top steps at her friend's house.

After we went inside her girlfriend's house, I encountered several women moving throughout the kitchen. Somehow, I accidentally moved too close to one of them smoking a cigarette, and she burned my left hand with a lit cigarette. When I returned home, my grandmother asked my mother where my "good" clothes were and if she was proud of having dressed me up like a tomboy. I did not mind. Although I liked the feminine clothes my grandmother put on me before I left the house with her on outings, they were sometimes not comfortable.

My grandmother was distraught when she saw the burn mark on the top of my hand. She started screaming at my mother about why she had not been more careful when she was supposed to be watching me. She felt my mother and her girlfriends were careless when getting high, and she did not want me around them anymore. She feared I might get seriously hurt someday.

Not long after the cigarette incident, my mother returned to pick up the remaining belongings she had left in the apartment to make room for my grandfather Lorenzo's stuff. He was coming to visit us from Puerto Rico. It felt like he and my grandmother had somewhat of an estranged relationship, as if she resented him. It was apparent they were not getting back together, but for some reason, she was willing to help him out with a place to stay, clean clothes, and home-cooked Puerto Rican food.

My family spoke of Ponce, Puerto Rico, located in the Southern Coastal Plain region about three miles inland from the shores of the

Caribbean Sea and how great the food was on the island. Even though I never made it there with my grandmother or anyone else for that matter, there was never anything like tasting the food my grandmother put her love into when she cooked for us.

I always dropped whatever I was doing outside when I heard the sound of her voice calling me inside, signifying it was time to get ready for dinner after playing outside all day. When I reached the top of the apartment steps, I inhaled the delightful aroma of homemade "sofrito" as it fried at the bottom of a pot of rice or beans and permeated through the building. It was a base sauce made with garlic, onions, peppers, and herbs such green recaito and cilantro, which she used to make a pot of red rice and beans.

The best meals she made consisted of "arroz con gandules" or habichuelas," which were sometimes red kidney beans simmered in a mixture of fresh minced garlic and Goya's Sazon seasoning mixed with tomato sauce. It was usually accompanied by well-seasoned and crunchy but moist fried chicken, pork chops, or steak with onions (Bistec Encebollado), which she cooked until the meat was tender and juicy. I always hurried inside in anticipation of the flavorful and filling dinners.

Every year, we looked forward to Parrandeando, which was a tradition of going from house to house, dancing, drinking Coquito[32] and eating "pasteles" for Christmas and New Year's Eve holiday dinners. Enjoying pasteles during the holidays was a Puerto Rican tradition, which began by seasoning pork while separately bringing a large pot of salted water to a boil. The pork encasing, made from green banana masa, was placed inside the smashed masa, which was wrapped in banana leaves and dropped in to boil gently for over an hour. It was a special time of year when our family could savor every morsel of pasteles after tongs were used to remove them from the water, and the outer parchment discarded as the banana leaf wrapping was not edible. We usually ate it with a side of "arroz con

---

32 A creamy coconut rum drink

gandules." I would put ketchup on my "pasteles" to make them even yummier.

While she cooked, my grandmother was always accompanied by the energetic personalities of the Spanish Radio Program, "Radio Borinquen." In between the ballads, salsa, and merengue, their fast talk filled the air as she blasted the radio on high volume. She listened to it daily while cleaning and making breakfast, lunch, and dinner.

On days when she picked up her Department of Public Welfare (DPW) Public Assistance disbursements, we would walk to a high traffic Commercial District to Four Sons Pizza. Although it wasn't Puerto Rican food, I looked forward to those trips to Four Sons Pizza at 2308 North Front Street. It had been my first experience tasting authentic Italian cuisine, at least it was the closest to it in my neighborhood. The sauce was just the right amount of sweet between the foundation of flavorful cheese and a crunchy crust. Pizza quickly became one of my favorite meals whenever we went out.

During the weekday mornings, my grandmother fed us milk and cereal or eggs and bread for breakfast. My grandmother enjoyed her green tin can crackers resembling unsalted saltines and yellow labeled Bustelo coffee she made with lots of milk and sugar after putting it through a strainer made of cloth.

When my grandmother needed alone time, which wasn't too often, we watched cartoons like Tom and Jerry, Bugs Bunny, and Popeye. Even though I lived in a Spanish-speaking household, English felt like my predominant language. I was able to write, understand and speak English much better than I did Spanish. I spoke slang Spanish when speaking to family members who spoke little English.

My grandmother enrolled me in, and walked me to, preschool classes across the street from Hartranft elementary, on the south side of 9th and Cumberland Streets. I assimilated seamlessly. I never needed any English-as-a-second-language classes. The time I spent in an American preschool and watching Sesame Street was instrumental in my learning. I was always eager to show her the new words, phrases, or numbers I learned from Bert and Ernie, Big Bird, Cookie Monster, The Count, and Mr. Snuffleupagus.

Sometimes she would let all of her youngest grandchildren climb into bed with her to watch game shows like the *Price is Right*, *ABC Channel 6 News* and her soap operas, *All My Children*, *One Life to Live*, and *General Hospital*. It always felt great and I seemed to be the happiest.

It was my grandmother and grandfather who, during a brief visit, expressed a ton of joy over my early childhood accomplishments. They bragged about me every time they heard great things from my teachers when I was dropped off or picked up from school. I remember the joy I felt when my grandfather visited with us and how happy I was being accompanied to school by adults. My grandfather was always glad to see me after school. I was equally happy to see him and watch him walking along my grandmother's side.

I practiced writing my name, numbers, and most of the letters in the alphabet and could not wait to show them what I learned. Grandpa Lorenzo would be just outside the classroom doors in the designated pick-up area waiting for me after school. A couple of times he carried me back home on his shoulders. When we reached the top of the apartment steps, I smelled the pleasant aroma of my grandmother's homemade food.

When she remained home, he would try to warm up to my grandmother when we walked in from school, yet she rarely reciprocated. By the end of the season, he was on his way back to Puerto Rico. He gently kissed us goodbye, and I never saw him again.

I wondered what kind of life he was living in the "campos[33]" he described while he was with us. I pictured rural life with a lot of space in between the houses, fences, and land not far from the clear water beaches under the hot blazing sun where he would go back to live out the rest of his days.

---

33 Fields, countryside

Chapter Six
Breaking News

"Where you used to be, there is a hole in the world, which I find myself constantly walking around in the daytime and falling in at night. I miss you like hell." ~ Edna St. Vincent Millay

I never met my father's parents. My maternal grandmother, Catalina, who the entire family called Mami, raised me until I was almost seven years old. Fortunately, she was in charge during my imprint years filled with mostly positive memories of the caregiver who, despite not having much in life, was disciplined enough to make sure she created a stable, loving home for two impressionable young children. Throughout the fall of 1978 and spring of 1979, I excelled in school and attended church at St. Edwards every Sunday morning with my grandmother.

As a devoted Catholic, Catalina (Mami) believed the first holy communion was an essential part of our upbringing. The event consisted of a ceremony intended to mold our thinking and shape our identity as a people of God. There were lessons about being redeemed by the blood of the Lamb. I had a great deal of difficulty comprehending the concept of Jesus' sacrifice. I did what was requested of me and did not mention my confusion to her at all.

My grandmother was looking forward to seeing me walk down the church aisle in my stark white lace dress. I could envision her face looking at me as I made my way to the priest. He would facilitate me symbolically partaking in a ceremony by drinking cranberry juice from his cup and sucking on a broken piece of cracker in a reflection of Christ's sacrifice until it dissolved.

After a long, hot and slightly-humid summer day in July of 1979, we had company and my brother Javier was outside while I was upstairs changing into my pajamas. He was playing with a guitar my grandmother bought from a neighbor earlier that week when the neighbor walked up to him, pretending like he was going to show him how to play it. As it turned out, the neighbor was an addict.

The same man who cleaned himself up and sold the guitar to my grandmother was now trying to take the guitar away from my brother Javier. As soon as the man pried the guitar from his small child-sized hands, Javier ran upstairs to tell my grandmother what happened. At first, it was unclear if he needed medication from his asthma pump.

On that ill-fated Philly night, once my brother hurriedly completed his rendition of what occurred, the strong-willed fifty-plus-year-old Puerto Rican woman opened the front window and started shouting at the man. She demanded the immediate return of the guitar to her grandson or her money back. He refused, and her heart rate rose steadily.

The more she hollered, the worse it got and when he refused to return it one last time, she called him "Tecato", and "Maldito" before slamming the window shut. These were two terms are commonly used to describe druggies and those who engaged in illegal activity.

After she slowly backed away from the window, my grandmother sat down on her rocking chair to catch her breath. Moments later, neighbors banded together to pick up and carry my grandmother's heavy and immobile body down the apartment stairs. After a bit of commotion, she was in a neighbor's car. Shortly after, I was staring out the car window still in my pajamas as the vehicle made its way down Germantown Avenue, headed east toward Episcopal Hospital.

Even though the hospital was barely a mile from our apartment on Germantown Avenue and about a five-minute drive, it felt like hours making our way to 100 East Lehigh Avenue.

Once we arrived, we were told to sit inside the car and wait for news about my grandmother. Those hours felt like days. Then the air got colder after someone came outside and delivered an update that would shake the foundation I relied on to its core. I was in complete denial. A few short days later, I was instructed to walk up to her casket and kiss her goodbye. I hesitated and thought it could be a mistake. That's not her body. She's not dead.

The whole scenario was utterly foreign to me, and I didn't know what to expect. I walked over closer to her lifeless body and paused. I was unsure if she would come back to life.

After being prompted to continue, I mustered up the courage to position my lips towards her cheek. When they landed on her skin, her face felt like an ice-cold rock exposed to zero-degree weather. For the first time in my life, I was devastated. Unbeknownst to me, there was no way of getting around expressing my grief. I held it inside like I did when I heard news of my grandfather passing away. But this was much more of a challenge to overcome. I couldn't believe the doctors at the hospital could not save my grandmother's life.

I never considered what my life would be like without my rock.

We took it for granted that she would always be there for us.

Who would care about our well-being like she did?

Sadly enough, after that massive heart attack stole my grandmother from me, no one would ever care for us the same. There would never be another person in our lives like this woman.

My mother was now challenged to take responsibility for her children. She proceeded to raise us with limited maternal instincts.

Chapter Seven
Breaking Tradition

"Whenever you can't balance what you see with what you believe you have conflict." ~ Shannon L. Alder

When my grandmother died, my mother was finally forced to raise two children with an inheritance derived in the form of my grandmother's furniture and our public assistance disbursements.

She did not shower us with hugs, kisses, consistent care, and feeding. Her attention was focused elsewhere while we lived in a perpetual state of uncertainty with little sense of security.

As a seasoned addict, she ignored our basic needs while fulfilling her own. Her addictions worsened as time passed. The physical and psychological anguish was the result of intimidating gestures, and verbal threats too quickly followed by extreme action. We had both hidden bruises and those in plain sight. It was a total shock to go from the culture our grandmother shaped for us to the one formed by my mother. Dealing with rules of the new order was a daily challenge. It was even harder because they were always in flux and changed on a whim or whatever was convenient.

Despite her occasional frustration, the orderliness and predictability my grandmother Catalina provided in making the inside of our home a safe and inviting environment was now succumbed to my mother's compulsions. This woman, who abused substances most of her life, would rarely connect with us. Shortly after she entered our vicinity, we would experience the unpredictable nature and consequences of her severe mood swings.

While she was out, or in deep daytime slumber, my brother and I would take turns jumping out of the 2nd story bathroom window onto an old dirty mattress. If my mother was inside, we had to be careful because we never knew what mood she would be in when she woke up. If she was out, one of us had to be on the lookout. If we got busted jumping out of windows as a form of entertainment, we would get a beating. When we were doing something we probably shouldn't have been doing, it was best if we were invisible when she made her way out the front door or back to her bedroom again.

My brother and I were always unsure as to how she would be feeling, acting, or overreacting on any given day or night. I had watched enough television and been around my grandmother enough to know this wasn't how it was supposed to be. I was angry at my mother for not having the mental faculty to realize she was supposed to take care of her children, which is what my grandmother had done.

One day, shortly after my grandmother died, my mother pummeled me because I suddenly had to go to the bathroom while outside playing but no one came to the front door of the apartment building fast enough to let me inside. The cause was a beating for not being able to hold my urine long enough and having an accident on the stairway.

Living in poverty was bad enough. Living in poverty with a volatile single parent who was physically abusive and negligent was downright tough.

The main benefit of arriving at school before the first bell rang was free breakfast. A favorite item was a rectangular-shaped oatmeal bar I would wash down with an orange juice drink made primarily of powder mixed in water, placed in a small container. At lunchtime, I wondered if anyone at school realized it was rare to have all the recommended food groups in one meal a day, let alone two of the three recommended daily.

The health teacher talked about how important it was to eat the right food groups daily. I wondered if this person had the slightest clue about the lack of say-so we had regarding the food brought into our household. Requests or choices during my mother's reign were nonexistent. We ate what she brought home; no questions asked, period. I could not be in denial or lash out because this was, in fact, a new world order. If being silent brought a single moment of peace, I would go about my business and remain quiet as much as possible.

One Saturday morning during the summer of 1980, while my brother and I were watching Wonder Woman, Superman, and Batman cartoons, my mother walked into the living room and announced I needed to get ready because we were leaving the house soon. She disappeared into her bedroom.

After I finished getting dressed, I came back downstairs and sat next to my brother, who was watching "Kung Fu" movies. I thought it was weird how their lips were never in sync with the words. When my mother reappeared, we departed. We headed to the beauty parlor, which was near 5th Street and Somerset Streets. Instead of taking the time to wash and condition my hair before attempting to put a brush or comb through it until the tangles were set free, she decided to rid herself of my wild unruly curly hair, or at least as much as possible.

It was starting to get longer, and as a small child, I had no idea what to do with it, and neither did my mother when it grew well past my shoulders and down my back. She looked at a few pictures at the hair salon and pointed to a television star's image with a cut short all over, blown-in on both sides, and feathered toward the middle of the head. I thought it looked beautiful in the picture. But I wasn't

43

convinced the style would look good on me. My mother thought it would look better than my ponytail styles. She would not help me care for my hair after my grandmother passed, and I would not dare to question her authority on the matter for fear of getting a beat down.

I was motioned to sit in the chair that a woman had just vacated after having her hair washed. I reluctantly replaced her, and my head was pushed back into the sink while I was seated. After some significant shampooing, rinsing, and conditioning, a towel was wrapped tightly around my hair, and I was motioned to sit in another chair. Soon enough, the hairdresser was going to chop off my relatively long curls, which I was dreading. I wasn't old enough to style my hair.

I made a mental image of how my hair looked when my last annual school picture was taken and silently said, "Bye hair. I'll miss you, a lot."

It started to dawn on me; nothing good would come from this attempt to tame the hairs on my head. I froze when the scissors bumped against my neck, and my wet curls began dropping onto the floor like spiraled winter snowflakes. My heart sank every time a curly flake hit the ground and dried up on the floor beneath my feet.

I got a little depressed when I saw how short my hair looked.

I tried not to fidget while the hairdresser took almost an hour to blow dry and curl my hair section by section, making sure dry hair did not overlap the wet hair as it awaited its turn with the hairdryer. When it was all over, I was given a mirror to see the back of my head. It looked like Billy Dee Williams', aka Lando Calrissian, in the *Star Wars* film advertisements on television. I didn't look like the picture in the hairstyle binder.

On the way home, I was beginning to admire the softness in my hair and how I was able to run my fingers through it. When it was curly, my fingers would inevitably get stuck in my tangled dry curls.

It wasn't long before the summer heat, and east coast humidity started to take its toll on my new hairstyle. The more I sweated, the more my hair shrank inward into frizzed up patches, which first appeared at the base of my roots and closest to my scalp.

By the end of the night, I had done so much running around the block, jumping rope and playing hopscotch, my hairstyle had miserably fallen apart. It looked nothing like it had a few hours earlier. Before getting ready for bed, I washed my sweaty hair in the bathtub.

After I finished taking a bath, I looked in the mirror and saw a wet poodle staring back. The next morning, I combed the dry curls out into an afro. I had no hair products or tools to style it differently, so it remained as is, a kinky hot mess.

When I went outside to play, the Puerto Ricans that moved on the block earlier that summer were ruthless with their comments about my kinky hair, and they were relentless in teasing me daily. "Look at your ugly afro!" they hollered from across the street. I tried not to let it bother me, but it was hard to ignore. Sometimes I heard it, ran inside, and did not want to come back out to play. I did not want to be around children who were trying to make me feel inferior.

Maritza was my aunt Santa's youngest daughter. Out of all my cousins, I felt she was the one everyone treated the best. At the time, I thought it was because she was the prettiest in their eyes. She had long light brown straight hair, a bright skin tone and, European features. She was the one they would pick to be part of wedding parties and events, something I never had the opportunity to experience as a child or teenager. I wondered how wonderful it might be to have such good looks and to be so popular.

I never felt pretty enough. I suppose it was due to the way her mother and father treated my cousin like a prized possession relative to the rest of us. My mother liked her own afro, but as a child, sporting one was not the best look for me. She had no idea the new neighbors' kids were making fun of my hair. I missed the ponytails my grandmother styled my hair into when she was taking me outside.

Suffice it to say, as a child, I didn't like the afro. Didn't she realize the 70s were over? I was a just a child and it was the beginning of a new decade. Saying anything about it would be useless, so I settled into a new state of affairs and said nothing.

Chapter Eight
Breaking Up My Fire

*"The predator wants your silence. It feeds their power, entitlement,
and they want it to feed your shame." ~ Viola Davis*

L ess than a year after my grandmother passed away, while
walking unsupervised to Hartranft Elementary School, I was
shoved into an abandoned house between 7th and 8th Streets
within a few feet from Cumberland. The building was located
directly across the street from my school. I do not recall how
I ended up there, but I remember my brother catching up to me
somehow and walking in on my perpetrator. I can only attribute him
finding me to God's divine intervention, which stopped the deviant
dead in his tracks.

I look back on the incident as if it were an out-of-body experience
where I could see him stepping away from my body as he
discontinued further attempts at sodomizing a child who was
unaccompanied as she made her way around the hard-knock streets
of North Philly. Back in my own body and mind, there was an
extreme feeling of disgust and utter humiliation.

The incident shook me up. My fire didn't die out, but it was
broken up, and the flames shrunk down to the smallest level they
could be while remaining lit without requiring a burst of oxygen.
This traumatic event incited the formation of a personal code of
silence. I managed to keep my fire minimally lit, but the look inside
my eyes would never be the same again. Bringing it up would not

enact change on anyone's part.

At the time, I could not fully comprehend how fortunate I was to have escaped before the sexual assault turned into something much worse, well beyond the cruel intention it was already. When I got home, there was no one around to notice anything different about me. I did not display any distressing behavior. Nothing good would come of discussing the elephant in the room with my brother.

My grandmother was the only person I would have been able to trust with my thoughts, care, and well-being. Up to that point, aside from learning the art of self-care with trial by fire outcomes due to my grandmother's departure, this was the most traumatic experience of my entire life. I vowed to myself to keep the sordid details hidden. I buried the deep-rooted horror and never shared that I had an encounter with a sex offender when I was seven or eight years old. I didn't ask my brother to call the police, no one filed a police report, and tragically, the pedophile would likely continue running rampant, preying on little girls on their way to school.

I decided it would be best if I just pretended the elephant didn't exist. If I wanted to survive and perhaps maybe even one day thrive in an unfair world, I had to stop myself from sharing the reality of the dark world I was exposed to. I had to become disciplined. I had to depend on myself to get up on time, get ready, and cautiously make my way to school with both eyes wide open. I had to be keenly observant of my surroundings with a raised eyebrow when things seemed suspicious. I had to be ready to move with the swiftness of a cheetah when I was within the realm of clear and present danger.

Nearly everywhere I went outside of school or work, I was known as China. After this incident, China became more than a nickname; it had to become an alter ego. China is who I would summon to survive the streets of North Philly.

Chapter Nine
Breaking Bread

"The hunger for love is much more difficult to remove than the hunger for bread." ~ Mother Teresa

I t wasn't all bad growing up in Philly. My mother had her good days, but they were rare. It felt like most of the time there was drama in the air and I'm not talking in an award-winning kind of way either. During one of those less than 20% of the times when things were going well, I remember my mother listening to her salsa, jazz, and soul music in her bedroom, which we could hear all over the apartment.

Although I heard music coming out of the record player and the radio, most of the time, the source was usually behind closed doors in the isolation of her bedroom. I could hear the lyrics to songs like *"I Will Survive"* by Gloria Gaynor and *"One Nation Under a Groove"* by Funkadelic. My mother loved music and told us the music spoke to the heart like no other art form. She delighted in most kinds of music, except for country, unless it was Dolly Parton or someone more mainstream as the years passed.

I enjoyed watching "Soul Train" and developed an early love for music and dancing to songs. There was *"Rapper's Delight"* by The Sugarhill Gang, *"Funkytown"* by Lipps, and the song that made me want to be loved more by the Pointer Sisters/Sister Sledge called *"We Are Family."* Whenever I heard it, I secretly wished I had sisters to bond with, to do my hair and help me feel more like part of an actual member of a family. Or at least someone to join me in coming up with creative long-term escape options as we grew up.

Although older, my brother was more oblivious to our problems or at least that's what it seemed like on the surface when we were younger. I often spent a great deal of time as a child analyzing our problems and desperately trying to think of solutions.

On a particularly good day after my grandmother's passing, I felt special. There weren't any issues to think about, and my mother looked great physically and in spirit.

It was October 11 of 1980, and I wondered what Anita, as my brother and I called our mother by her family nickname, would do for my birthday. It was disheartening that she hadn't done anything I could recall the prior year after my grandmother passed away. My brother must have told my mother about my feelings about my last birthday and spending it in her girlfriend's house watching television, which we did daily.

But that year was different. At midday, my mother walked into the apartment with a white cake and pink trimming. She bought a pink number eight candle, and decorations. I don't know if she made any of it, but there was also food and drinks.

She smiled throughout the day while enjoying herself at my eighth birthday party in our apartment. Things seemed almost normal. Like most people, she wasn't the most attractive when she was angry or frowned, but when my mother smiled, I thought she was beautiful. She had dimples like Mario Lopez, and I could see how my father had fallen in love with her after they met.

I will never forget my eighth birthday because I can't recall anything to that scale ever being done for me on my birthday as a child ever again. My mother, our family, and her friends all danced in the living room to salsa, merengue, and songs like *"Ladies Night"* by Kool and The Gang. They swung their arms around while shaking their hips back and forth, trying to stay in rhythm with the music as their feet moved to the beats. I was excited about the celebration and felt nothing but love as I watched our family get together in my honor.

I did not dance well to Spanish salsa and merengue but I enjoyed trying. I had fun that day. I even spent a bit of time outside listening to disco songs on the street, pretending to be a pint-sized afro-haired diva rolling around on blue and yellow sneaker skates I got as a gift for my birthday. I had a great time listening to my mother's new Diana Ross record, as I sang along to the lyrics of *"I'm Coming Out"*.

Before going back inside, I tried to move like Dorothy Hammill on ice skates, even though I had roller skates. The rest of the kids danced in the living room while the adults stayed in the kitchen, drinking alcohol and reminiscing about old times. They did their best not to get out of control as they did at almost every adult get together.

This one time, in honor of the day I was born, everyone seemed to be having a drama-free time. Anita was wearing black leather pants and a short-sleeved red bodysuit. My aunt Blanca was wearing black pants and the same top Anita had on but in black with a thin brown belt wrapped around her small waistline.

My aunt Santa had on a long white wrap skirt with a black and white long-sleeved patterned top hugging her chest and waist in all the right places.

They hugged each other and posed for pictures, sharing their grins with the person in charge of taking the photo. It was a picture I would grow up to appreciate, cherish, and frame.

Even though Anita was drinking more than anyone else, laughing a lot and making faces leading me to believe she may have had a bit much to drink, no one offended her in any way.

Despite the fact my initial cut and style blow out had transformed into an afro, which I could not tame, my eighth birthday was the best gathering I had ever experienced growing up.

There was **no better feeling on earth than being loved by family and friends.**

Chapter Ten
Broken Heart

"It is a fact that I don't get enough love, I never did get enough love"
~ Nina Simone

Once the night turned into morning, things went back to our new normal under my mother's regime. We settled into sadness caused by many waves of abuse and neglect. Not long after my birthday party, my mother came home after being out all day and caught me accidentally spilling some powdered lemonade. It made its way from the counter onto the kitchen floor. It was dark. I panicked when I saw her coming through the living room into the kitchen. Out of the corner of my eye, I glanced at her and recalled how senseless her beatings were in comparison to when my grandmother whipped us. Mentally beating myself up about having made such a clumsy mistake delayed my ability to move fast enough to clean up the spill in an acceptable and timely manner.

Before I could take any action to make the evidence disappear, she sprinted toward me. I was terrified. She grabbed my little hands, turned on the stove, and held them both close to the fire until one hand grew a giant bubble filled with a clear liquid over the top. I started screaming within seconds of being exposed to the flames. But the sounds of my agony didn't snap her out of her trance. How could a no-impact accident warrant such violent consequences? I was too young to understand the condition of being bipolar or what it meant to suffer from the disease of addiction.

All I knew was, the more my hand ached, the more resentful I felt my grandmother was gone, forcing us to live with this lunatic. I wished I could be more like Kelly or Sabrina from "Charlie's Angels." They never failed at escaping their captors or someone always came to their rescue. My mind wandered into the land of the Bionic Woman and Wonder Woman. These women seemed to have an extraordinary amount of speed. The Bionic Woman ran fast enough to get away and Wonder Woman could raise her hands to block body blows with the power of her unique wrist bracelets. Sadly though, I was not a superhero. I had no means of protecting myself. I had to deal with the fact those were television shows. None of those women were ever showing up to save me.

Shortly after my hand healed, some of the kids my brother hung out with invited him to play. Not wanting to leave me home alone, we made our way down the street to the park. I enjoyed the geometric dome climber, train, and monkey bars and time spent outside like healthy children.

Even though we took the risk of leaving the house without my mother's permission because she was either out or in deep daytime slumber, thoughts of her wrath were never too far behind. For the most surprising reasons, this woman would often lose control of her mind, causing the rest of us to deal with the aftermath of her insanity.

In retrospect, the life I had known under my grandmother's guardianship was like living in an alternate universe. Even when grandmother disciplined us, most of the time, I felt she was teaching us respect for self and respect for others. If I stepped out of line, I would immediately be checked and put back in my place.

The most extreme my grandmother ever got with me was when I was about five or six years old and finished taking a bath. With only a towel wrapped around my body, I was on my way to my bedroom upstairs when I heard laughter in the abandoned lot next to our apartment. Instead of going directly up the stairs, I made a left detour and leaned onto the window sill in the kitchen.

Moments later, my grandmother quietly entered the kitchen from her bedroom. On this hot summer day, I got busted attempting to get the attention of one of the youngsters out in the lot. In my small childish mind, I was not doing anything wrong and only saying hello.

But my grandmother must have sensed what was going on from her bedroom, and she appeared in front of me like a Ninja. She sized me up, stared me down, and proceeded to slap me from the front of the kitchen window into the bathroom. When her lesson ended for the day, I was instructed to promptly get dressed before taking my behind upstairs to my bedroom. Lesson learned, never lean into window sills with only a towel as a body covering.

In comparison, my mother's beatings were lacking in logic. Most days, we were hypnotized by whatever was playing on the television. As latchkey children, after we arrived home from school, did our homework, and made ourselves something to eat, the television screen would become our babysitter. The actors were our companions. They helped us cope and distracted us from reality.

The summer my hair was battered, I went to church with my brother weekly to finish preparing for our first communion, which my grandmother initiated. I wasn't even ten yet, and I was frightened the humidity was going to take a horrific toll on my bangs before we had any pictures taken to capture the memory of my first communion.

I recall my mother trying to make an effort for the event, as she put a little bit of makeup on and bought a dress she wore with slightly heeled pointed-toe shoes. It was a rare moment in time when she showed up in feminine attire.

I never saw my brother dressed better. He wore a crisp white suit with a black collared shirt and shiny black shoes accompanied by a big cheesy smile complemented by his dark-haired Afro. My short bangs had shrunken up a bit and my partially blow-dried hair was hidden in the back under a white veil covering. I was excited to have on a white dress. I twirled around in front of the church before going inside. My mother shot me a look. It put an end to my movements. It signaled the risk of getting hurt if I continued.

A few weeks later on Halloween night, my mother bought us some cheap plastic face-masks. She dressed my brother and me up in some old thrift store clothes ten sizes too big because the idea was to make us look like homeless bums. To support our wish to trick or treat, she gave us brown paper grocery store bags. We knocked on the neighbors' doors south of Germantown Avenue, past the Ile Ife Museum on the corner of Dauphin Street, and back up to York again.

My mother's attempts to be a near-normal parent, although welcomed, were always short-lived. After our first communion and the trick or treating outing, things were back to our new normal. My brother and I resumed responsibility for ourselves. Our meals were made of the cheapest ingredients my mother could find when she managed to go food shopping. On the positive side, the lack of structure and limited oversight meant we developed self-reliance.

My mother was too consumed with herself to notice much at home and the risks associated to breaking up with a dangerous lover. My brother and I would witness the damage to her heart at the hands of someone who did not like the idea of parting ways.

While still trying to convince her to move on, things did not go as my mother had planned. Her ex-lover followed her to a bar and would not accept that their relationship was over. When she started pleading with "Billy Boy" to take her back, my mother departed from the establishment. Unbeknownst to anyone, her furious ex-lover followed her home. This woman previously told her no one else would be with her if she ended the relationship, and she tried to make sure of it—similar threats I would experience years later from an ex and ex-husband.

Not knowing the lady was seeking revenge for being rejected, my mother stood in front of the apartment window. Somehow, that woman swiftly crept up behind my mother with a knife in her hand. My mother must have felt a presence in the room because she immediately turned around. It was too late, though. Although this woman meant to take my mother's life by stabbing her in the back while she was looking out the window, she ended up stabbing her in her chest. Miraculously, my mother survived this horrendous ordeal and returned from the hospital with a twelve-inch scar between her breasts that ended near her belly button. Embedded across her chest were horizontal scars across a vertical scar from the knife entry.

The hospital staff told my mother what they had done was a temporary fix, and she would have to return for additional surgeries. However, not long after her scar healed, she was back out in the streets without any thought of the risks associated to her behavior. Sometimes, we would not see her for more than 24 hours. When she stayed still long enough for us to be near her, we could hear the sounds of the artificial heart valve ticking non-stop inside her chest cavity. The ticking sound from her chest sounded similar to the hands of a clock. It was unclear how long she would live. At one point, she was not expected to make it beyond my middle school years. I always wondered about her health and mortality. We did not have an ideal mother-daughter relationship, yet she was all we had in the world.

Chapter Eleven
Breaking Our Spirits

"Honor yourself for all the ways you learned to take care of yourself during your abuse" ~ Jeanne McElvaney

After my mother got stabbed in the chest, we moved from the three-bedroom apartment on the 2300 block of Germantown Avenue to a small row home off the corner of Dillman and Tioga Streets, in the Fairhill neighborhood of the city. It was in the eastern region of Philly, made up mostly of Puerto Ricans mostly bounded by Broad Street to the west, Front Street to the east, York Street to the north, and Cecil B. Moore Avenue to the south.

The move to the 3400 block of Dillman Street, Philadelphia, PA 19140 was a six-minute drive away from our old apartment. This decades-old brick row home was on a small street, tiny in width and barely fitting an SUV, let alone a school bus.

Our new place to live had a single bathroom upstairs to share with others within 1,008 square feet of living space. Unlike our old neighborhood, this one was made up of very few African Americans with more Puerto Ricans and more whites than I had ever seen in my life, except on television. The majority of the white kids in the neighborhood lived on the East side of Front Street toward the letter streets started with A Street, past Kensington, Frankford, Aramingo, and Richmond. Most African American kids lived on the West Side of 2nd Street, where the numbered streets began, and this population increased in numbers the further west and south of Broad Street.

The majority of Puerto Ricans lived in between the two groups dominating the vicinity surrounding 5th Street, nearby "el bloque de Oro" (The Golden Block). No one with a hint of color in their skin was welcomed east of Front Street. White flight was real in the early 1980s and those who could not afford to leave were often resentful of our existence. There were tales in the hood of the hazards many encountered when finding themselves on the wrong side of a street, avenue, or boulevard.

Growing up on the wrong side of Philly also meant limited opportunities for legit work as factories began to shut down. Not only was learning how to take care of yourself at a very early age a given for many children but so was learning to hustle, which usually occurred before puberty. My first job was unpaid and bestowed upon me in 1981. It was selling weed for my mother out of our home.

My mother's unwritten rule and verbally communicated policy was always to get the money first. Only then would one of us head toward the weed hidden in our grandmother's old record player, encased in what looked like a rectangular shaped wooden box with a lid on one side that was raised to play records. Although a bit younger than my brother, I was chosen to complete steps in the standard operating procedure which occurred after taking the money and before giving out the weed.

At the age of eight, I had a conceptual understanding of the process and the associated inputs, customers, outputs, and suppliers. My mother, the boss lady, was a supplier to neighborhood pot smokers, and she had suppliers of her own who provided the product, which served as an input to service the demand created by local customers.

My mother made many poor choices when it came to her children, but she saw I was born with natural abilities that included, but were not limited to, math. It was a critical skill to have if you are running a business with the only form of payment being cash. My job duties consisted of exercising caution while collecting money in a sale, not to mention the most crucial task, counting correctly to secure a profit when completing each transaction.

Key terms in the family business were joints and nicks. We learned five-dollar nickel bags were called nicks and sold in a tiny mustard color paper envelope containing enough marijuana to make seven to eight joints. Each joint was filled with weed and rolled up in thin white, nearly see-through Top paper about the size of an adult finger. Depending on the person rolling it and how much weed they placed inside, the joint would either be slim, regular-sized or a fatty. The price for a regular joint was a dollar.

A tactic to move the product quickly was to offer customers a better deal by selling a nick for five bucks because, that way, they could get more joints for the same cost. With nicks there was more product for less money but required the customer to roll up their joints. It was a simple matter of whether they were willing to put in the labor effort and minor cost of Top paper for an increased return on their investment.

A customer knocking on the door triggered the order to the sale process. The step after confirming if they wanted a nick(s) or a joint(s) was to take the money first, then immediately close the front door, count it, hide the cash, grab change if needed, grab the right amount of weed, and hand it to the customer. Timeliness of exchange was critical, as it was important for everyone's sake to send them on their way as fast as possible.

I was self-motivated to make sure I met job performance standards, even though I was not compensated for being a dependable worker. I was compliant and always did what was expected of me, demonstrating a quiet competency. Refusing to complete the task of handing an illegal product to potentially dangerous customers in exchange for cash never crossed my mind.

I didn't think of it because I lived in fear of my mother and what she was capable of when it came to her punishments. When the delegated responsibility of selling weed came to an end, I got my first paid side hustle, tutoring other children on the block for five dollars. Early in life, I learned wanting money to buy take-out and snacks meant earning it.

With her friend in tow, my mother routinely made her way up to the Unity District; always on time for regularly scheduled visits to the County Assistance Office. The location was assigned to our zip code by the Pennsylvania Department of Public Welfare. I was rarely taken along for the visits, which I never complained about because when I did go, my mother would have me speak on her behalf. I despised being forced to sit up in someone's face practically begging for public assistance and a range of free services, including food stamps and government cheese.

During a memorable trip to the Unity District, we were left without adult supervision to wait in the car while my mother and her friend walked north a few blocks to the welfare office. Out of pure boredom, we left the car and climbed the trees nearby. As soon as we saw them getting close, we got back into the car, hoping we went unnoticed. We were so engrossed none of us was watching out for them. When they got to the car, we got a look meant to inform us that climbing private property and knocking off light bulbs, as we made our way down the trees, warranted a beating.

It was a long quiet car ride back home. As soon as we arrived, my brother and I were led to the basement and handcuffed as my mother prepared to beat us with a knotted brown extension cord. When the beating was over, she took pictures of our marks and bruises and dropped off the picture roll to get developed. After she picked up the photos, they were blurred and creepy, as if there was a ghost in the room.

Chapter Twelve
Breaking a Sweat

"Never be bullied into silence. Never allow yourself to be made a victim. Accept no one's definition of your life; define yourself." ~ Harvey Fierstein

When I started 4th grade at Cramp School on Howard and Ontario Streets, I would not get the warm welcome I got from my African American brothers and sisters who taught me the proverb about it taking a village to raise a child. At Cramp, the racial tension felt heightened among multiple groups, unlike Hartranft. The majority of the whites looked down on and resented the Puerto Ricans and African Americans who moved into their neighborhood.

It was like living in Archie Bunker's neighborhood from the television show *"All in the Family."* All it took was an episode or two and it was apparent Archie's views were those of an ignorant bigot who loved his family but was challenged by his prejudices. Like Archie, these neighbors did not want us moving into their area.

To my surprise, I was greeted at school by an African American girl whose facial expression made it clear she was not a fan of the new girl. This surprised me considering the sense of tribalism I experienced at Hartranft. I was a curious child and did not hold back when I needed to ask questions for clarification or answer a question asked of the students by the teacher. I felt threatened by her evil grin, and more so when she lifted her two fists against her eyes, looking back at the clock and gesturing with her hands that after school, she'd be taking care of me.

Sure enough, at the end of the school day, no sooner did the bell ring than I found her rushing toward me with her friends in tow. I jetted out of the schoolyard, running as fast as I could to make it the few blocks back to my house without getting caught. I was out of breath, and angry this bully was chasing me home for reasons I didn't understand. I wanted to rest then confront and question her, but she didn't appear open to rational thinking, so I kept running.

They were all on my heels and gaining on me. I was sweating profusely and wondered if they caught me before I got to my steps, would the girl crush me or pound on me while the others held me down. It felt like I had a hole in my side, and the pain wasn't letting up. I pushed forward and continued until I finally made it home. After I managed to unlock the door and get safely inside, I slammed the door right in front of their faces. I was relieved my mother wasn't home because I knew she would have made me go back outside and fight. She had a lot of heart and told me stories of being chased and fighting back regardless of how many chased her around the city.

For a brief moment, I felt like a character in the action movie *"The Warriors,"* a 1979 flick about a crew being chased down by gangs in an urban city. Except I was a crew of one, and the gang situation was not so dangerous. We were in the third or fourth grade, and I was unjustly harassed by someone who wasn't quite Luther, a man who clicked beer bottles together in the movie while hollering "Waaaarrrrrriiiorsss, come out to pla-ay!"

The next day, I found out the girl's nickname was Pumpkin, and it made sense because she looked exactly like a round fat scary Halloween pumpkin. For a brief second, I thought about reasoning with her about why it made no sense for her to target me, as I had done nothing to justify her actions. I just wanted to live in peace. I had enough going on at home.

During the lunch break, I ate my free school lunch and mulled over whether I should confront her, fight her to prove a point, or ignore the entire event as if it didn't even happen. I walked over to her table, but she did not have a receptive look on her face. Before I could say a word, the bell rang, and she walked away. Pumpkin never said or did anything to me again.

Due to things becoming worse on the home front, I was more independent than ever. By early 1982, due to what my grandmother would have called "jibara" and "tequata" tactics, my mother "lost" all of our furniture and belongings she inherited from my grandmother. We were on the move again. We ended up moving in with my mother's girlfriend and her two kids, who lived two blocks down and one block over from the house we rented on Dillman. It was another row-home on Philip Street between Allegheny Avenue and Westmoreland Street and the rent payment was $140 a month.

Our walk there with black trash bags in hand was about five minutes southeast. We couldn't afford movers, so we had to carry some of our stuff to another leased low-income row-home. My mother and her friend figured it was best if the two of them combined four children into a slightly bigger three-bedroom, one bath row-home with approximately 1,146 square feet of living space in the Fairhill neighborhood. They could afford to split the rent and utilities, which wasn't much more than a couple of hundred dollars a month. I randomly thought about how I was living in what was called the Fairhill neighborhood, but little associated with living there seemed fair or had any real hills.

After moving to Philip Street, I joined the school choir. The music teacher said I didn't have the same type of voice as Nel, a Soprano. But she said when both of us sang, the blending of our voices was harmonious. Nel was a musically talented girl who could sing higher notes. I was an alto with a stronger middle voice good at hitting lower notes. I continued to inquire about the distinctions until the matter was put to rest when I found out the soprano usually brought forth a brighter sound quality compared to the darker alto sound. How symbolic of my dark, troubled life. And no one could deny the fact that Nel could sing her butt off. She could be a successful lead singer if she ever formed a band or decided to become a solo artist.

Nel reminded me of a Puerto Rican Janet Jackson (the *Good Times* Janet Jackson) with long beautiful straight hair. We walked each other home after realizing we lived seconds from each other. She was an only child and I didn't have any sisters, so we immediately became friends on our first walk home. When we reached my steps, I noticed her book bag tucked in the corner of my front porch. Apparently, my older brother had taken it from school earlier in the day. I apologized to Nel profusely after I saw it and while handing it back to her before she went home.

Little did my brother know the girl whose bag he stole lived on our block and would become my friend. She lived on the corner directly adjacent to Allegheny Avenue in a two-bedroom apartment. Her grandmother resided in the first-floor apartment beneath the apartment she and her mom shared after her parents divorced. Her parents both worked to provide her the kind of life neither of them had growing up in Puerto Rico. She was the richest girl I had ever met because she had everything she needed, wanted, and more. Her mother and father both contributed to buying her some of the cutest clothes, toys, albums, gadgets, and a Nintendo game system that we played Donkey Kong after school and on weekends.

I also looked forward to when she shared her after-school snacks like Pop-Tarts. I tore into those sugar filled pastry snacks when we got hungry from dancing around her living room. She had legit cable television, something we would never have in our home. Having utilities like electric and gas were difficult enough to maintain, and a phone line was never a given.

One day, my mother brought home a stray dog, which was surprising, considering she didn't make much effort to take care of her children. Before the day was over, I ended up finding a tick stuck to my stomach, sucking my blood. I thought that was disgusting. After I yanked it off and killed it, Nel knocked on the door. In an instant, my day got brighter.

She thought we should do cheers for the neighbors and eventually, the children at St. Christopher's Hospital. We went from door to door, telling everyone who invited us in that we were doing cheers. A handful of residents donated a few quarters to each of us. We collected less than three dollars before we heard the ice cream truck nearby. That venture, suffice it to say, was short-lived.

Because I didn't have caring parents at home who took an interest in me, I was always glad when Nel knocked on the door so we could hang out or get going to school. School was a place where teachers and counselors took an interest in me. I was labeled "smart" in comparison to my peers. It felt good. Unfortunately, they also noticed when I arrived at school wearing thrift store clothes reeking of kerosene.

By the fifth grade, my mother would neglect not only her children but also utilities for months on end. Sometimes, we had to light candles to see at night. Other nights, when the heater was not working, we slept downstairs with the oven door open and the stove range burners on to get some heat going into the contained living room area. When the gas was shut off, we used electric or kerosene heaters to stay warm in the winter. When the electric was on, but the gas turned off, we used a hot plate to warm up food and boiled water to take lukewarm baths in shallow bathtub water.

It was a major hassle running up and down the stairs with hot water and repeatedly pouring it into the bathtub, hoping it would not get cold before I finished boiling the next pot. Once it was deep enough, I had to wash quickly before the bathwater turned frigid. I dried off even faster because the freezing temperature would cause the cold air to hit my wet body, making it quite uncomfortable.

I preferred using the stove to stay warm because it was not a pleasant experience hearing the words kinky stinky when the smell of kerosene clung onto my clothes and cloth-covered book bag. No matter how much I tried, I could not get rid of the smell. It didn't matter if I washed them by hand with soap and water or if I machine-washed them with no-frills detergent, the odor was too strong to remove, and a foul and a constant reminder of my home life.

In the wintertime, when the temperature really dipped, we'd cover up with as many blankets as possible and watched television closely huddled together. We had a floor model television we could see but not hear sound from and a thirteen-inch television we put on top of it because it had no visual, only sound. My brother and I would switch both TVs to the same channel and sit close together, taking turns darting toward the small television and back to couch after shaking the metal coat hanger we had taken apart to make an antenna to improve the reception. We also got creative with pliers to change the large television channels when the channel knob broke off. Remote controls were not part of the equation in our homes back then.

The winter I turned ten was particularly rough. It was also the winter my mother's roommate signed up her two children to receive a Salvation Army hosted dinner and toy drive. They were not able to attend. Since my brother and I were a boy and a girl of about the same age, my mother had us go in their place. We ate the free meal, which tasted like it was free because of the weird after taste. We took home donated toys so my mother would have one less thing to think about at Christmas. It was a strange and rather awkward experience. Albeit appreciative, I could not find it enjoyable.

In between school and visits to Nel's apartment, the neglect continued. At age ten or eleven, I tried to jump a fence in my backyard on Philip Street, and one leg got stuck on the fence while the other landed on the concrete in front of it. To say I was in pain was an understatement. I called out for my mother, who was preoccupied in the basement and took her time getting outside to examine the cause of my shouting. Once she got me inside the house, my foot swelled up pretty bad, so I asked her to take me to the hospital. She replied by loudly letting me know she would do no such thing.

Instead of seeking medical attention, like I had hoped she would, she roared at me in Spanish about how lucky I was that I didn't break my neck. She told me to put ice on it and go lay down. That night, like most others, I cried myself to sleep.

After my mother stopped selling weed, she would send my brother and I down two blocks north to the playground where a local gang was forming, not to play but to pay for some personal consumption weed. We would get her a nickel bag, which had gotten smaller since the time we were selling them a couple of years earlier. Now, they only contained enough weed to make exactly five skinny joints.

I recall many days coming home from school when she sent me across the street to the speakeasy to get her a couple of White Mountain Coolers or non-flavored Malt Beverage like Colt 45 and Old English 800. Getting her "medicine," as she called it, was about copping[34] a nickel bag of weed and forty ounces of alcohol so she could lock herself up to get a decent high or buzz going on without having to deal with the outside world.

Before I turned eleven years old, I desperately wanted to earn my own money. I was tired of not having decent school clothes, so I stepped it up a notch and took a partially legit summer job selling pretzels from plastic crates on various intersections throughout the city. I state somewhat legit because even though it was perfectly legal to sell Philadelphia Soft Pretzels, I was not of legal age to hold

---

34 Buying

a job. I learned about the opportunity after buying soft, warm hand-twisted pretzels with an overlapping knot at Cramp school.

They were inexpensive at 4 for a $1, and it wasn't too hard to scrounge up loose change so I could get one with mustard for a quarter. Because my inquiring mind always wanted to know, I asked about the possibility of selling pretzels myself during the summer. I teamed up with a vendor who pushed pretzel carts on numerous street corners throughout the city. I was among a group of children and youths who had no problem going out there to earn extra cash this way. At the start of the summer, I carried baskets of pretzels for sale in the heat as I walked up and down city streets. I sold them in the Castor Gardens neighborhood in the lower Northeast section of Philadelphia and at the Pathmark Supermarket at the intersection of Aramingo Avenue and Ontario Street in Port Richmond.

By August, some of the kids living on the north side of the block saw me selling pretzels. They'd eventually call themselves the ATT gang, for "At The Top" because they earned money to look dope by slinging dope a block north of where I lived at the corner of Philip and Ontario Streets. They were tough kids with designer clothes and lots of gold jewelry. Part of me wanted to be like them and hoped they would let me hang out with them one day. But alas, those hopes were crushed when they started calling me "Pretzel Girl."

Although they were cordial to me later in life due to mutual friends we shared over the years, whenever they saw me traveling to and from the corner store, school, laundromat, or to the Chinese takeout restaurant, they hollered in my direction "Pretzel Girl." It was embarrassing. I ignored it and kept going about my business.

At times, I wondered how selling drugs was acceptable but selling pretzels was something to be ridiculed. In my child-like mind, a hustle was a hustle, and a product was a product. I never gave too much thought to the teasing. Instead, I would go into my house and blast the radio. Songs like *"Kids In America"* by Kim

Wilde would come on, and I could relate to the lyrics... "Looking out a dirty old window…"

I realized children in this up and coming Badlands neighborhood could be mean—real mean. Besides being chased home after school on my first day at Cramp and labeled for selling soft pretzels, I was starting to get teased about my mother's masculinity and the fact she never appeared to have any male lovers come by after my father's death. Everyone living so close together made it almost impossible for neighbors to stay out of each other's business.

What they did not know was she never got over the loss of my father, the only man who ever truly cared about my mother. He was a hardworking and caring man who I was informed had a genuine love for her, and when that chapter ended, she went into full-fledged natural-mode.

By this, I mean, she was no longer going against her natural attraction to the same sex. She stopped feeling ashamed and stopped suppressing. Instead, she chose to be herself when it came to her attraction to women and came out well before society was accepting of it.

When I didn't want to be alone with my thoughts anymore, I would go down the block to Nel's apartment to listen to her new Olivia Newton-John album. We would role-play, lip-syncing all of the album's most popular songs in her living room. There were many dramatic moments when we heard a favorite, "Physical," and jumped around before her mother and grandmother got home from work.

My brother and I were unsupervised the majority of the time and practically raised ourselves, like most children of addicts. We got up from bed on our own and made it to school every day alone. We made our way with other kids who lived in the neighborhood, whether it was by their side or in direct line of sight.

We ate whatever we could find. We dragged our dirty clothes to the laundromat, bathed and went to bed on our own. These activities started when we were quite young. As a teenagers, not much changed.

Chapter Thirteen
Breaking Ground

"Many abused children cling to the hope that growing up will bring escape and freedoms..." ~ Dr. Judith Herman

During the week, going to school brought solace. It was where I excelled. It was the closest thing I had to normalcy, even if it was only in one aspect of my life. I was eager to leave the house in the morning and did not look forward to coming home afterward. Despite what was going on at home, I looked to positive reinforcement from my teachers at school.

In 6th grade at Cramp Elementary School on Howard & Ontario Streets, I was advised to spend time considering options after graduation. Before graduating from sixth grade, I was told to really think about where I would attend middle school. Going to Stetson Middle School on the corner of B and Allegheny, like many kids in the neighborhood, was actively discouraged.

The drop-out rates there were high, the academic track record was low, and lack of student discipline was scary. My brother went to Stetson as a pit stop before dropping out in the 12th grade. He left Stetson with poor grades and suspensions for various things like stealing walkie talkies from the teacher's assistant. After all the trouble he got into, he made it to his senior year at Edison High, Stetson's high school counterpart. Sadly, he dropped out with literally a couple of months left to graduate.

Because I had the potential to meet the criteria for magnet school admission, I wanted to go to school as far away from where I lived as possible. I was encouraged to attend Conwell Middle School, located at 1849 East Clearfield Street, two blocks from the Kensington and Allegheny bus stop and El train. It was referred to as model magnet school. I asked about other magnet school options. I heard about Amy 6, which at the time was located on Chew Avenue in the northwest area of Germantown Avenue. Due to its distance, it seemed to be a better option. I also thought this magnet middle school would have students from diverse cultural backgrounds who would be more accepting of each other. To get there, I knew I had to get up even earlier and catch two buses and a subway train to get to school. Conwell was closer to the bus stop by my house near 2nd and Allegheny and just one bus ride away. In the end, I applied to Amy 6 and was accepted for fall admission. I spent the summer of 1984 singing the lyrics of *"Girls Just Want To Have Fun"* by Cyndi Lauper, all while holding a broom mic in my hand.

At eleven years of age, I arrived in 7th grade, enthusiastic about the future. It was there I met Ms. Dorothy Page, a teacher who would encourage my learning and growth. A woman who saw my potential and told me what I desperately needed to hear, delivered as tiny periodic bursts of oxygen to keep my fire lit. When I doubted if I should remain after the first year, she didn't tell me what to do. She listened to me when I told her everyone who was attending school there but living in my neighborhood was going back. We developed a relationship that was so close, I told her to call me "China". She wanted me to make my own decisions about what was best for me and I took note of her tone and body language. I decided to stay another year and graduate from Amy 6.

In the 8th grade, a couple school outings included a visit to the Liberty Bell and a trip to Washington, D.C. These events added to the many positive memories of my time spent at Amy 6. Attempts to share this positivity with my mother, or to show her how well I was doing in school, often felt like epic failures.

My high level of performance in school did not prevent ongoing abuses. At a time when soft drinks were not sold in plastic, she threw a glass Pepsi bottle at me while in a moving vehicle. It caused a massive lump behind my ear. Another time, she beat me so hard with a metal broomstick for something I didn't do that I blacked out and woke up wondering how she could hit me so hard I could no longer see the light of day while the sun was still out.

Growing up, I did not know about religion. Like Jill Scott responded when asked if she was religious, I wondered what else existed. I thought about how it had all gotten to be so complicated and the people so judgmental. I had days when I could relate to the Buddhist need to chant. Then there were times I wanted to holler and shout like a Baptist. Before graduating from middle school, I took a handful of my brother's asthma pills, and my mother had no choice but to make sure I got to the hospital. Some attention was better than no attention, but it came at a price. When I got to the hospital, the staff thought I was faking about taking the pills. After being adamant that I was not pretending, I was forced to drink a charcoal-based concoction, which tasted like mud. That day, I learned liquid charcoal makes you throw up and gets whatever is in your system out of your body. After repeatedly gagging until I barfed up the gray matter with the undigested contents in my stomach, they sent a psychiatrist in to assess me. I reassured the psychiatrist there was no need for concern. I said I wasn't faking but was not trying to kill myself. I stated I wanted to live and was merely making an attempt to get my mother's attention. For whatever reason, after two or three sentences, I was discharged. What I didn't say was my mother was an addict who abused and neglected her children, and this is what I resorted to in order to get her to actually see me and change.

My mother played lottery numbers almost daily, and if she won, we were hardly aware of it. But not long after the asthma pill incident, she won a few hundred bucks and surprised us with a trip to the sneaker store to get some fresh kicks. I was ecstatic to pick out a

75

pair of size 6½ red suede Pumas. I wore them with everything. It didn't matter if they didn't match my outfits. I felt confident in my Pumas when I bounce-walked around the neighborhood. I wore them until the suede faded so much the original bright red was very faint.

I wore those red suede Pumas to visit the Philadelphia High School for Creative and Performing Arts (CAPA), a magnet school in South Philadelphia. I thought CAPA was like the school on the television series "Fame." Irene Cara performed the title song of the same name, and I saw a bit of myself in Coco Hernandez, a character in the television show. I wished I could develop the talent to act, dance and sing like she did. Actually, in my mind, I did. When I was home alone and cleaning, I role played and sang along to the words, "Baby look at me and tell me what you see. You ain't seen the best of me yet. Give me time I'll make you forget the rest. I got more in me, and you can set it free." I adored Debbie Allen and watching her play the role of Lydia Grant on "Fame," I wished she was a member of my family. She was caring while holding her students to high standards. She drove them to greatness through actions and words delivered seriously. She meant business when firmly stating, "You want fame? Well, fame costs. And right here is where you start paying. With sweat."

I had a keen interest in Creative Writing, Music, and Acting, but I had doubts about being able to make a living in any of these spaces. I never thought I had the Hollywood look or the support to succeed in any of the related professions. I told myself if I was smart, it would be easier to attend another magnet school with a smaller chance of failure. I felt it would be much easier to leverage an academic experience as a means of escaping the Badlands, one day.

As a result, Central High was a top contender. Throughout the city, Central was known as the premier public magnet located in the Logan section of the city. The criteria for entry included minimum standardized test scores in both Reading and Mathematics, report card subject marks for the previous two years indicating all "A's" and "B's," an excellent behavior record, and an attendance rate of 90% or better, with a minimal number of late arrivals. Demonstrating exemplary attendance, punctuality, and behavior were foundational factors in gaining entry into the institution. Check, check, check, and check. Similar to most magnet schools, it wasn't enough if I wanted to attend. I also had to submit a handwritten essay. What would I write to secure a spot? What could I share from my own experience that wasn't too much? Graduating from this school could serve me well in overcoming poverty.

Thoughts of graduating from "the crowning glory" of Philadelphia's public-school system led me to believe it was a realistic route to earning scholarships. The possibility of becoming a Spanish-speaking attorney as a means of breaking the badlands and doing good for myself and others swirled inside my head.

I also reflected on the fact that in 1984, Sheldon S. Pavel, an educational pioneer, became the principal of Central High School. In the face of protests, a judge ordered the school to admit female students. The school was breaking new ground and had only started accepting girls a couple of years earlier after a drawn-out court battle ignited by a few Jewish teenagers who sought admittance to the impressive institution. Two years later, under Dr. Pavel's leadership, the school had become more culturally diverse. I was granted acceptance as part of the growing "Hispanic/Latino" population. At the time, this population barely made up ten percent of the city's total population, with the majority living in and around the Badlands.

Early on, I learned to navigate my way around the city on foot as well as via Southeastern Pennsylvania Transportation Authority (SEPTA). Since the age of eleven, whenever I used SEPTA as a means of transportation, I'd be reminded of the demographics outside of my neighborhood. By the time I reached high school age, I was an expert and resourceful at taking buses, subways, trains, railway lines, and trolley bus services in and around Philadelphia.

As I looked out of bus windows, I came to see Philadelphia was a multicultural city made up of what felt like a ton of neighborhoods. With my own two eyes, I saw the majority of my African American brothers and sisters lived in places like Germantown, West Philadelphia, Mount Airy, and South Philly. The Spanish-speaking ones lived in Fairhill, Juniata Park, Hunting Park, Kensington, Frankford, and Olney. I hadn't yet met any that lived in Society Hill, Center City, or Rittenhouse Square. The highest concentration of Philly's Spanish-speaking population was Puerto Ricans, with a sprinkle of Dominicans, Colombians, and Cubans taking up residence on and near the vicinity of 5th Street.

I had been working for several years before I was able to present my mother with a form requiring her signature as evidence of parental permission to work without breaking any child labor laws for those under the age of 16. The summer before I started high school, I came across and applied to work in a program supported by Philly's first black mayor, Wilson Goode. It was working for the Philadelphia Anti-Graffiti Network, a non-profit organization.

My earnings were a whopping $214. Although it was hard work repeatedly rolling paint over spray-painted walls in hot and humid conditions, with the heat of the summer sun piercing its rays through my body, I was well on my way to becoming a productive contributing member of society. I was a city youth who was paid minimum wage to cover graffiti-covered buildings serving as visual reminders of the city's everyday life in places like The Badlands, whose occupants kept its gang legacy alive and well. Most of us felt a real sense of accomplishment in the community, especially doing our part to cover walls with fresh coats of paint. While it didn't combat the spread of graffiti long-term, at the end of each day, the temporary effects and income did some good in our lives. Then we'd return to the job site after painting and find walls were immediately redecorated with new tags to make sure everyone in the neighborhood recognized who the artist was and their affiliates.

Chapter Fourteen
Broken Dream

"If parents want to give their children a gift, the best thing they can do is to teach their children to love challenges, be intrigued by mistakes, enjoy effort, and keep on learning. That way, their children don't have to be slaves of praise.They will have a lifelong way to build and repair their own confidence." ~ Carol S. Dweck

I was looking forward to being welcomed into the second-oldest continuously public high school in the U.S., which was founded in 1836. As a new student traveling from North Philly on my way to the school building on the corner of Ogontz and Olney Avenue, arriving was like entering a whole other world. I would soon learn most things in life were relative. High school teenagers at Central High were more advanced and equipped with resources beyond my reach. The student body was made up of mostly by middle-and upper-class teenagers who wore named brand clothes and accessories purchased with discretionary funds. Funds, I'd never have working part-time minimum wage jobs. While I wanted to proudly wear clothing that would make me feel like I fit in, I needed money for SEPTA tokens, not a burgundy Central High School sweatshirt or T-shirt with mustard yellow lettering.

Unlike the building I walked into every weekday morning, I was much more than a little frayed around the edges, and it showed. I struggled to keep up. I used some of my last few summer job dollars to buy thrift store Guess jeans. My money was running out and being chosen by the administration to get past the front doors was easy compared to what it would take to make it all four years to graduation. I asked my mother for cash. Unsurprisingly, she had one excuse after another for not giving me any of the money she collected from the DPW on my behalf.

As time went on, she got more creative with her excuses, and eventually, she started saying someone assaulted her, but it was only on check day. I suspected she had spent the money to feed her cravings within hours of having picked it up. At first, she only claimed they stole her cash from her near the pickup spot. Then she would get more elaborate and transition from being robbed of money to also being raided for her food stamps. It didn't take more than a couple of inquiries before I realized any effort spent asking would be futile, as it was clear she was using the check and selling the food stamps to get high. I was distraught and started to redirect focus.

I was surrounded by people and relatives who had unhealthy compulsions tempted by the appeal of cash for those ready to enter or engage in the drug trade. I could barely make it to school without encountering evidence of the open-air recreational drug market symptomatic of a ruthless atmosphere where danger and chaos ruled. My route to school, wove around rotted, run-down buildings. I would pass miles of graffiti-covered walls and a multitude of abandoned properties neighbored by poverty-stricken tenants. Aside from foster care as a means of involuntary departure for those under the age of eighteen, I felt my escape options were limited.

As a first-year student, it was difficult to deal with all the factors associated with growing up. Add to the mix apprehension that came from not being able to break apart from poverty. The experience created an unwelcomed and soul-sucking companion inside of me. I wished I could break up with it already. It didn't help that I no longer had the comfort level with academics as a fallback means of feeding my self-importance. On top of that, there wasn't much to eat at home anymore. For sustenance, I made my way to Nel's apartment or my aunt's house during mealtimes.

Before my teen years, my mother's drug use had not yet entirely steered her away from buying at least something minimal for us to eat every month. Most of our meals consisted of the same ingredients: some mixed meat, eggs, rice and potatoes. These were our primary source of nourishment. It varied in the presentation. On food stamp issuance day, she would buy a hundred-pound sack of rice, hot dogs or mixed meat patties, eggs, and potatoes. We cooked white rice and fried eggs for a carbohydrate and protein combo, or we would have scrambled eggs and French-fried potatoes. The eggs, hot dogs or meat patties would serve as a protein companion to the carbohydrates. Vegetables were out of the question unless she could get cans of corn on sale. Broccoli and asparagus were foreign to us and salads with any type of lettuce was rare.

Our meals mainly consisted of starches she would buy in bulk at a discount after getting her monthly food stamp allowance. This was taxing, but at least there was food at home. At the beginning of the month, we were lucky to have hot dogs, not beef hot dogs, but hot dogs made up of some strange combination of chicken, pork, and turkey. If we ran out of eggs or needed milk for cereal, my mother might send me down to the corner store to get more, which I dreaded because it meant paying with food stamps. I dreaded the lines.

If someone standing behind me saw the paper stamps, it was a sign of being even more dirt poor than they were, or that's what I imagined. Most of us residing in the area were living off public assistance, but there was a percentage of working-class families that made those of us on public support hate the thought of being caught paying with food stamps. At times, the glares were telling. By the time I reached high school, my mother's addiction heightened. She wasn't spending money on food anymore, nor was she sending us to the store with food stamps.

Going to Central exposed me to intelligent teens, many were Jewish or mixed half-white and half-black. Once, I was invited over a classmate's house after school. I was thrilled because not only did it make me feel a slight sense of belonging, if we hung out long enough, someone might offer to share a meal or snack.

Inevitably, during our off-campus outing, the question surfaced, "What are you?" I was asked at Amy 6 too. Those living in the neighborhoods of Upsal, Mount Airy, or Chestnut Hill weren't sure what I was as far as race. When I hesitated to respond fast enough, I would get "What kind of high yellow are you?", or "You a redbone." I didn't know the terms were used to describe a black person with a light complexion attributed to the high proportion of white ancestry.

During my high school years, I could see it but was clueless to the fact that most Puerto Ricans were in fact a people of mixed race. I responded with, "No, I am Puerto Rican." I had yet to acknowledge myself as a person of mixed-race due my limited insight on the matter and a lack of historical knowledge. I felt it in how I was treated and always hesitated to check off Hispanic on government forms. I could feel my mixed ancestry in my soul.

To satisfy my curiosity, I researched and learned Puerto Ricans are a genetically assorted people who did not descend from one racial group but a variety, with the original islanders being Taino Indians. They were the indigenous natives who greeted Christopher Columbus and the Spaniards on their infamous historical voyages. In all of my years of public schooling, even though it was an American territory won during a war, the history of Puerto Rico and how my parent's ancestors became known as Puerto Ricans was not taught in any classroom. I had no idea terrorists[35] claimed the island of Borinquen and renamed it, Puerto Rico, because in Spanish it meant prosperous port.

The fun times the natives spent playing and barbecuing with friends and family in the island paradise was over once the terrorists

---

35 People who use unlawful violence or intimidation, especially against civilians, in the pursuit of political aims

stepped foot on the island. Most of the original inhabitants were massacred, chased from the beach into the mountains and the remaining remnants relegated into subservient roles of servitude. Similar to West Africans and the Indians of North America, the land they had once peacefully occupied, and the resources used to sustain their livelihood was lost via a hostile take-over. All of which was rooted in racism, greed, and the belief one race was superior to another. Based on their appearance, they were not considered worthy of land ownership or human rights.

The majority of the Tainos were enslaved and forced into capricious acts against their spirit. Many who escaped murder, died due to exposure to different diseases. The survivors were enslaved and made to work in the island's goldfields. The terrorists' repeated visits would eventually lead to genocide. The Tainos who did not commit suicide when facing the facts regarding their options, survived and were absorbed into the new population. When their numbers dwindled, the Spaniards stole Africans off the west coast of Africa to compensate. The Africans were also forced into slavery and sexual acts against their will.

By the 1800s, the sons and daughters of sexual intermingling replaced the annihilated Taino Indian workforce as the Spaniard colonizers settled into the island along with other nationalities. Thus, we became a blend of predominantly Spanish-speaking but biologically Indian, African, and European mixed people. Much of this blended history is evident in independently published books and fact-based DNA tests. The only way they survived the transatlantic slave trade was by not letting the cruelest of circumstances break their spirit; this was an essential aspect of their lasting endurance and something I had to learn to do in life repeatedly.

Because of the island's precious resources, those in power within the United States of America didn't just want a piece of Puerto Rico; they wanted all of it--and all of it by any means necessary. Like the Europeans before them who engaged in terrorism, they followed the playbook for hostile takeovers and established a system of control based on lies and false promises to keep the people in a submissive state. When they were just about done torturing the Native American Indians, they found others outside of the United States to conquer.

It was interesting how the United States defended itself against Europe yet went to war with Spain for control over Puerto Rico. As a result, after four centuries under Spain's rule, Puerto Rico became an American war prize in 1898. Many of its resources were used and depleted by those in positions of power for over a century.

I knew in a group setting, we were like a box of chocolates, and you never knew what you were going to get. What I wasn't aware of was the mixing of races among the island's natives being the root cause of drama in some households. Controversial conversations about the island's history, statehood, and features showing up in one generation and skipping the next would result in heated arguments.

In retrospect, I would imagine being a United States territory might warrant a bit of fact-based history-telling in public schools. Why? I understood I was an American Citizen because I was born and raised in the United States, but I had no idea Puerto Ricans born on the island became Americans in 1917 without ever having to step foot on mainland soil. They could be drafted into American wars and claimed as citizens. However, they did not possess full rights of citizenship because those born on the island could be killed in American combat but denied electoral votes in presidential elections.

Back in my current reality, I was keenly aware public transportation was not free, I barely made it through my first year of high school and had to start seriously looking for a job. That summer, I worked at a laundromat at the intersection of 2nd and Ontario Streets, making about $40 a week for thirty hours of labor. I asked for that job one day when I arrived there after lugging clothes in a metal cart up the steps and realizing they were busy enough to hire help.

Because minors under fourteen years of age were not legally supposed to be employed nor permitted to work in any occupation unless they were performers in the entertainment field, I got paid cash under the table-meaning untaxed. As a result, I felt I was taken advantage of a bit. But I looked forward to paydays when I would collect my money from the laundromat owners who also owned the Chinese takeout restaurant across the street from the laundromat. I would grab a chicken wing platter, save some money for SEPTA tokens and go shopping for a cheap outfit.

My sophomore year was strained by the events happening at home. The way I processed it all in my mind was detrimental to my academic performance. I was called into the administration offices to explain the delta between the good grades I managed to get in ninth grade and the poor grades I was getting in the tenth. Although I had seen Dr. Pavel's friendly face around the building, I felt no more comfortable sharing my back story with him than I was with any of his appointed counselors. I felt none of them could ever relate to me or my circumstances and begging meant I never really belonged.

After taking a seat, I heard the words spoken to me throughout most of my school years, "You have the potential to do something with your life." They were usually followed by the dreaded question whenever I was asked to come down to someone's office. The inevitable question arose, "Is there something happening at home?" I wanted to fire back with a question of my own: "Where do I begin?"

I thought about saying, well, I am glad you asked, as I have much to get off my chest, and this might be better and cheaper to accomplish than robbing a bank or going to therapy. You see, after catching the bus westbound to Broad and Erie Avenue, while waiting for the subway headed north toward Broad and Olney, I hold my breath every weekday morning to avoid inhaling the smell of pure piss. Worse than that, I struggle to relate to the student body, and my absentee mother does not give me any money for clothes or toiletries, let alone for public transportation.

I have no support system. I have pent-up frustration, especially with my mother and eldest aunt because she is also my godmother. When my mother last got evicted, my aunt reluctantly took me into her home next to a house on the corner of Hancock and Cambria Streets. It is a small three-bedroom row-home she purchased in 1983 for about $10,000 due to property values decreasing.

The area has become extremely affordable because of the high crime rates, drug deals, and gunshots heard all day and night. Many evenings after forcing myself to fall asleep, I am awakened by "Pop! Pop! Pop!" sounds followed by the sounds of sirens. During the day, people like myself who are not involved in the drug trade cautiously tread past crime-ridden corners to get to and from our homes.

Recently due to seemingly backward logic regarding my cousins' behavior, my aunt rid her household of my presence and dropped me off at what appeared to be a forsaken squatter house on the 3500 block of North Randolph Street. I say squatter because it would have been evident to anyone entering the house that it was a place where my mother and her friends had been living without paying rent.

It was difficult to fathom why my aunt would drop me off with a black trash bag in tow as if I was a piece of garbage. Couldn't she see the place she was leaving me looked uninhabitable and my mother did not care about anything other than getting high daily?

Drug interventions in my family are unheard of as a means of helping family and friends. Children are apparently disposed of when they become a daily reminder that things are not well with a family member who is unable to take care of themselves, let alone their offspring. I manage to get myself to school every day; I am not sexually active, and I try to remain unseen most of the afternoon before I lay my head down at a decent hour every weeknight to get up early for school. It'd be great if a relative felt compelled to provide a roof over my head that wasn't slowly collapsing.

While still being probed, I imagined saying all of this in my head and momentarily thought I should keep it real in my response. Then, I wondered, what did they expect to hear? How would they react? Aside from getting me connected with a social worker, they were not going to be able to swoop in and save me from my circumstances. I heard a pause between a line of questioning and mustered up the courage to share a little about having difficulty getting to school. Shortly after, the principal authorized a donation of SEPTA tokens so I could travel via public transportation. It was good news.

I was grateful for the dedication, commitment, and leadership Dr. Pavel exhibited in assisting me with my situation. But it was overshadowed when I got off the #47-bus stop and arrived at the squatter house on Randolph Street. In an instant, my heart sank when I witnessed my mother smoking crack. The term "reality bites" would have been an understatement when it came to my home environment. I could not think of a single positive thing in my life and only focused my thoughts on the negative cards I was dealt.

I was angry, sad, and depressed about being born into a shit hole in an uneven playing field — a place where displacement was relentless. I had spent my entire life moving from one blighted block to the next while attempting to survive within a 3–4-mile radius of some treacherous cold-blooded streets within the same distance to and from the famous Independence Hall and Liberty Bell.

I began entertaining thoughts about being destined to do less regardless of the SEPTA token contribution. I was hungry and felt broken inside because I didn't want to live in a run-down, abandoned building with drug paraphernalia and empty alcohol bottles in and around it while watching my mother getting high. It was hard enough to make it in the hood with married parents that both worked, whose primary purpose was to love and take care of their children, but this family portrait or lack thereof only caused me to wonder if I could ever really amount to something more. What I walked in on that afternoon cracked me. I felt like giving up.

My self-esteem plummeted to an all-time low. I felt worthless. I managed to stop crying long enough to feel like I was starting to fall asleep but not before entertaining thoughts of being cut from the same cloth as the woman who, at my age, had reached and remained on a figurative Loser Lane. I seriously wondered what the point of continuing to force myself onto Ambition Avenue. It didn't seem worthwhile anymore and just felt like too much fruitless effort.

Against the odds, I had already become one of the first females to be accepted into Philadelphia's most prestigious public school, Central High. But now, as a sophomore, I was inching closer toward the certainty I would never graduate with a high school diploma, let alone make it to a high school prom.

I ended up at Wil's again. Weary of the conditions we were both born into, we regularly silenced the noise that consumed our minds due to the lives we were mixed up in by partaking in a joint, blunt, or flavored malt beverage beer, which did not taste good but seem to calm us. All it took was a few sips or puffs before we exhaled some senseless drama, even if only for a brief moment in time.

Usually, we'd laugh at the silliest of things, get the munchies, eat, and try to fight off the sleepiness that instantly followed. This time, I just closed my eyes and asked myself, why was all this happening to me? I wondered, how on earth did I get here? My life had become more surreal than ever. From what just went down, it was my lifelong need for security and stability I had to problem-solve.

Running away was how I fathomed getting my biological need for human survival met. I had no idea where I would end up. I just knew it was time to roll out. I would soon be on a mission to find someplace to live where both my physiological and safety needs were not an issue so my mind and body could work in unison.

Chapter Fifteen
Broken Innocence

"The cruelest prison of all is the prison of the mind." ~ Piri Thomas

S oon after, I received news that Wil was being admitted to
Episcopal Hospital. During my visit, a Spanish-speaking
administrator probed into my life in front of Wil's hospital bed.
He was curious about her life and then inquired about mine.
Before I had the chance to say a word, she proudly told him that I
was attending Central High. He wanted to know more. I shared more
than what I had shared with the staff at Central High.

I didn't know what his end game was when he offered me a place
to live in a sought-after and safe South Jersey home. He claimed he
would make sure I had the means to get to school, with the only
condition being that I graduated. He must have sensed that I wasn't
too trusting of people and their ulterior motives because he invited
me over for dinner. I was curious so I accepted. He picked me up,
and we traveled about 20-30 minutes to the blossoming suburb of
Cherry Hill. I met his wife and enjoyed a warm home-cooked meal.

We traveled back to Philly, and we exchanged pleasantries before
I was dropped off. Given my background, I wondered why a grown
man would take in an at-risk teenager without having a hidden
agenda. To say I was suspicious would have been an understatement.

I tried to logically think through my options on which devil to
live with, the one I just met and didn't know at all or the one living

on the 2800 block of North Lee Street. I pondered the pros and cons. The latter pressured me to have sex with him in his mother's basement for months on end.

Like many people who wanted to escape from Philly, there was a choice to be made about what part of New Jersey I would live in; in my case, it was either Cherry Hill or Mays Landing. Would my new reality include living among well-intentioned strangers? Would my feet rest on cushioned mauve-colored carpeting with expensive padding while I did my homework and watched Yo! MTV Raps, which was being released that summer?

Going back to the 2800 block of North Hancock Street wasn't an option anymore. My aunt made it clear when she last discarded me that I could come by and entertain myself there while patiently awaiting remnants of her home-cooked meals now and then. But I wasn't allowed to sleep over or list her home as my residence.

The abandoned house on the 3500 block of North Randolph Street she took me to live in just a few short months ago felt like a slight step above being homeless. I felt like an insane squatter there who repeatedly arrived home from school, expecting my mother to responsibly welcome me in with kerosene heat and edible food in the kitchen. Matters with my mother were worse than ever.

How could I think about continuing my education at Central High and establishing a legitimate career path out of the ghetto? All I thought about was getting through each day without losing my mind and my mother to crack. Because of my mother's antics, I had already spent most of my life worrying and mentally exploring how to depart from metaphorical Despair Drives. I didn't even have two years of high school under my belt, and the reality of having to determine what tristate area home I'd live in confronted me. Staying in Philly at the time was too depressing.

On April 15, 1988, I made my decision to move to Mays Landing and shack up with my boyfriend. That was also the day he took me to Center City to see the movie *Colors*, starring Sean Penn and Robert Duvall, two of the most talented actors I would ever watch on screen. The trailer we saw before deciding to see the movie was action-packed. Not quite yet a full-fledged movie buff, I had grown to appreciate many types of films and wanted to check this one out because the story seemed as real as the complicated stories in my own life.

Wearing the matching stonewashed apparel he bought us, we held hands as we walked from his house on Lee Street past the sounds of chaos and booming car stereos toward the El train at the intersection of East Somerset Street and Kensington Avenue. It was hard not to notice the prostitutes and heroin addicts who had become permanent fixtures in this apocalyptic terrain. They were visible around and beneath the elevated train tracks.

Once we made our way up to the platform, I walked to the edge of the train tracks. I stood there, contemplating my future until the approaching train heading south to 15th and Market screeched to a full stop. There were few words between us on the ride. He didn't have much to say, and I didn't want to talk about what had occurred. When the train reached our destination, we found a diner near City Hall and grabbed a bite to eat before walking to one of the multiple movie theaters within a four-block radius.

After ordering a soda, popcorn, and chocolate candy, we made our way beyond the thin industrial carpet and onto the sticky theater floors. In the back against the left corner wall, we found two seats with some privacy.

As I watched the movie, I compared the scenes to my everyday life and the environment in North Philly. The main difference was, the crime and violence where I lived took place on the East coast, and the movie took place in the streets of the West coast. Both were places where people seemed to be murdered almost every day of the

91

year, and innocent bystanders shot in the middle of the stupidest arguments. Both were places where people engaged in reckless and destructive activity due to local cultural mindsets.

On the way back to Badlands, I told my boyfriend that *Colors* gave me an increasing desire to break out of Philly. I just had to do it in a way that allowed me to still pursue an education, support myself, and achieve my dream of losing my virginity after wearing a stark white wedding dress. He said his life was better with me in it, and he would permit me to attend school and get a part-time job, but he felt we were too young to get married. He tried to get me excited about attending Oakcrest High School in the fall. It was a public high school located in Hamilton Township, in Atlantic County, minutes away from the townhouse his parents just bought.

He continued negotiations by telling me what he thought I still needed to hear, given my state of vulnerability. I remember he used a combination of flattery and promises to convince me that there was no other shorty for him, and I was the only "jawn[36]" he wanted to make a life with outside of Philly. He claimed he was going to buy me an engagement ring. He declared his commitment by announcing that he had already secured his parents' approval to let me join them when they moved to South Jersey. We both knew that meant more than changing my address to his new residence in Mays Landing.

It also meant an inevitable fate-altering moment when I would complete the transition from an innocent girl in the hood into something else. I would not be eighteen for two and a half years. At least I knew him, I reasoned with myself. Thoughts about whether it was worth continuing any further efforts to hang onto my virginity for dear life crept into my head. Was it so unrealistic? I wasn't ready for my first sexual experience yet, but if it took place, two immediate words came to mind, "not painful," I silently prayed.

Feeling nearly powerless before reaching the end of my

---

36 All-purpose pronoun, in this case live-in girlfriend

sophomore year, I packed up the few belongings I had and left my mother's crack house on Randolph street for good. I moved in with my boyfriend into his parent's row home in the middle of a tiny street block to the east of Front Street off of Cambria Street.

I delayed the inevitable for weeks. During a visit to my aunt's house, her husband told my boyfriend to stop trying to get me to give it up because I was going to be just like my mother. I wondered why he would think such a thing. Just because my mother was gay, it did not mean I would be too.

My boyfriend, whose street name was Blitz, had hood-wifed me, which meant he allowed me to share a home with him even though we were not married. I dropped out of Central to live in his parents' basement on Lee Street. I didn't see any better alternative than moving in with them because living with the hospital administrator who was a stranger, felt like a weird thing to do. By the time summer started, we'd all be living in a newly constructed community out of state. Soon enough, I thought, I'd finally break out of the Badlands.

What I hadn't realized was that the weeks until the big Jersey move took place would be filled with more than trips to Great Adventure and the Jersey Shore. An overwhelming amount of energy was spent pressuring me into giving up my virginity. He knew it was just a matter of time before I gave up and gave in to his unceasing demands. I was grasping firmly to my virginity after a roller-coaster relationship with this part-time neighborhood drug dealer. After weeks of living in his mother's basement, it dawned on me that I had to give in to this boy's demands soon. Based on his "Blitz" persona's daily remarks, his hormones were growing tired of my non-accommodating presence.

I started to see how naive I had been thinking I could live there rent-free without finding a way to pay for room and board. He tried to make me feel at ease by always claiming he would take it easy and be gentle, but none of his words lessened the stress about the loss of my innocence at such a young age. I envisioned him shredding the only thing of value I had left in the world.

I wanted to wait until I got married to have sex, but after my mother told me to bounce[37] the day of the Coke can incident, the idea wasn't an option anymore. Even though I can say with a hundred percent certainty that I was not emotionally, physically, or mentally prepared and probably wouldn't have been for a long time, he would no longer wait. The truth was after I moved in with him, I had put my boyfriend into a real position of power over me.

About a month after I moved in, I realized how exhausted I was from the cumulative effort of fighting off the hands that continued to creep near my underwear. Like most young hormonal teenagers, I too, got excited when I was in the mood to make out. I was fine while we were fully clothed. I could feel the heat we generated when we kissed, and our bodies smashed together. But every time an article of clothing came off, my anxiety increased. I couldn't get into it beyond that point, and my mind drifted elsewhere. I felt an intense amount of pressure and didn't understand his need to pulverize my insides when I wasn't capable of going anywhere.

In his mind, weeks equaled a lifetime, and his patience had grown thin. One ill-fated Philly day, after chasing me into the basement, he managed to position his body on top of mine. I was out of breath from the effort I put into getting away and not turned on in the slightest by thoughts of him trying to forcibly penetrate me. He saw my facial expression and stood up. He asked if I was okay, and I replied, "yes," even though I was distraught. He proceeded to take off his white boxer shorts, and I gasped. When I looked into his face, it was apparent that I could not continue resisting. If I didn't give in, he would get pissed about blue balls again. I feared consequences.

It was time to go beyond the world of fully clothed heavy petting. In a matter of seconds, my boyfriend was now fully naked. I lay

---

37 Leave

94

there, almost frozen, in a submissive position, my mind numb. I was no longer resisting. I thought just keep going until the pain was unbearable or until it was over. Luckily, within a few minutes, the latter came first. I wondered what all the talk of it being such a pleasurable experience was about. I wasn't feeling anything but pain in more ways than one. After it was over, the bed felt moist, so I checked the sheets and found them drenched in blood.

My period was not due to arrive yet. I panicked at the sight of all the blood that was coming out of my body and soaking into the bedsheets. There was no feeling of euphoria as my cousin had described. All I wanted to do was get those sheets washed before the owners of the house came home. Definitely before any of them decided to come down to the basement to do a load of laundry.

After turning the washer on and placing some detergent inside it, I closed the lid and told him to keep an eye on it so he could put the sheets in the dryer as soon as the washer stopped. I sprinted upstairs to the second floor to get washed up and rid myself of the icky feeling. As the hot water fell on my head, I thought about how he had broken me, just as I predicted.

While he could not be blamed for sexual assault because I consented, the blood that continued to flow from my body sure did feel like the result of an injury, one I willingly engaged in. I wondered how serious I should take it when I was bleeding after hours passed, then days. Did losing my virginity mean I was now broken?

As each day passed, I grew more concerned. It wasn't just the occasional liner type spotting; it was nonstop, full-sized breakthrough pad bleeding. I went from seeming sure that it would quickly pass to doubting myself at every turn. Should I go to the doctor? Should I wait to see if it ended? Was this normal? After a week of second-guessing myself, I went in to see Dr. Williamson on Lehigh Avenue for his medical opinion about the bloody side effect of losing my virginity.

I didn't have any residual pain anymore or a fever, but we were moving out of state soon, and I needed a root cause explanation, not to mention a treatment to make the bleeding stop. After all, I couldn't risk the situation getting worse and my bleeding to death, completely missing my chance to finally escape gang society.

If something did break inside of me, I had to find out if the doctor could fix it. Fortunately, in spite of the bloody mess, the doctor confirmed that my fear of having my vagina broken to the point where it was unrepairable was completely unfounded. He calmly explained that although rare, my hymen must have torn during the brief moments of friction, but there was no need to panic. He wrote me a prescription for a pill to make the bleeding stop while providing another one for birth control pills.

Chapter Sixteen
Breaking into the Burbs

"There are opportunities even in the most difficult moments." ~
Wangari Maathai

A fter being on the road for a little over an hour, we arrived in Mays Landing in my new beautifully landscaped home community. I didn't give them much time to settle in and unpack before I asked his parents to take me to the closest mall, which was about a five-minute drive from their new house. I inquired about jobs and filled out what felt like twenty job applications over three-week period.

In addition to the Hamilton Mall, we ventured into the older Shore Mall in Egg Harbor Township, New Jersey, on U.S. Route 40/U.S. Route 322. Unlike the Shore Mall, the Hamilton Mall was a two-story mall encircled by parking lots, anchored by J.C. Penney, and competitors Macy's and Sears. Within the month, my persistence paid off. I secured a job at Kaybee Toy Store in the newly opened Hamilton Mall.

By the end of the year, my taxed income was $668. I wanted to earn my keep, so I gave my boyfriend's mother $25 a week to cover my living expenses. I didn't want to feel like a welfare case in her house. I put the little that was left aside for clothes and school supplies, knowing this year would be different. I would have to ask my boyfriend for some help since I was giving money I earned to his mother and shopping in my new environment was more expensive than what I could find back in Philly.

Even though I found a way to escape my mother's regime and was residing in a newly built Iacobacci community townhome in the safe and secure municipality of Egg Harbor Township, I wondered how long this arrangement would last. In comparison to living with my mother, I was still stressed, only to a much lesser degree. The choice I made in the spring to move in with my boyfriend and his parents by no means resulted in a drama-free living situation. That fall, in the briskness of early morning northeast coast weekdays, I would make my way toward the closest empty vinyl seats on a yellow school bus headed to the local high school.

As the bus passed miles of greenery made up of beautifully gardened landscapes, it stopped to pick up teenagers who never sat next to me. If they did, striking up a conversation along the way was the furthest from our minds. In the time spent on route to school, I thought about this new reality and whether my efforts to remain a part of it would last.

I often rehashed the past in my mind while stressing about the present. I had no clue how long I could take living in that townhouse. I stayed for reasons that included attending Oakcrest High. The school name was chosen based on its site on the crest of a hill, amid oak trees. Little did I know that once the bus dropped me off near my new home, I would once again find myself exposed to an antagonistic force. One that moved from Philadelphia but brought the Badlands mentality with it when relocating to South Jersey.

I had no idea the people I was now living with were some hardcore cocaine addicts. After sharing the same roof for a couple of months, I started to see behavioral and personality changes in all of them, each to varying magnitudes. The worst offender towards me was my boyfriend's mother who demonstrated more signs of agitation and irritability than any other member of my new household. In second place was her son, the seventeen-year-old who convinced me to move in with them under the guise of it being a safe environment for me to finish school and find steady work.

Due to their crazy unwarranted beliefs about my cheating or stealing, I do not recall ever being left in the house alone. Because they didn't know where to buy coke in Jersey, I had to accompany them on several trips to Philly each week to satisfy their constant craving for white lines, their drinking companion.

On the way to Philly, I tried to distract myself from the scenery by reading a newspaper or a book, but I always felt car sick within minutes. Staring out the window seemed peaceful until we arrived in Pennsylvania. As soon as the tires exited the Ben Franklin Bridge and turned onto 5th Street, the atmosphere quickly changed.

Repeatedly coming back to North Philly to be surrounded by inherently sad people and buildings fallen into disrepair made me realize, even though I had a brand-new roof over my head and clean, comfortable sheets with pillow covers to lie on at night, the situation was only slightly different. As the sedan headed north on 5th Street, it entered an almost mile-long stretch of roadway encased by concrete sidewalks labeled "el bloque de Oro." I thought about the irony of the words because in English they translated into the yellow brick road.

The further north we went into the city, the more the quality of the air decreased. It was a bit harder to breathe in an environment where so many residents were visibly conflicted by living in confined spaces while plagued by the problems of poverty. I dreaded arriving at the 5th Street bar up the street from Cayuga. I looked forward to them getting what they came for and heading back to New Jersey.

I don't know why I thought that after school started, the trips to the city would lessen. As a compromise to being practically forced to go to Philly on routine drug runs, I requested permission to get dropped off at my aunt's house, where I used to live and where my best friend Wil was still residing. They agreed and would turn right off of 5th Street and onto Cambria. When they reached the corner of Hancock, I'd usually look out the window and ask to be dropped off in front of the corner store. Shortly after, I'd walk across the street to spend time catching up with Wil while they left to get high. Getting to see and visit with her was part of the love in my love-hate relationship with Philly.

Chapter Seventeen
Broken Corner

"When we kill people, we feel compelled to pretend that it is for some higher cause. It is this pretense of virtue, I promise you, that will never be forgiven by history." ~ Shashi Tharoor

A couple of weeks after labor day, on an ill-fated Philly Saturday that fell on the 17th of September, I was back in the backseat of the gray sedan as it made its way from Jersey into Philly. I would never forget this excursion throughout the Greater Philadelphia Tristate area. It took place in an area recognized as one of the city's most profitable illegal drug superstores. At the time, drug dealers were selling Red Star cocaine in $10 dime bags marked with red stars to distinguish it from other brands sold across the city.

Because my roommates were selective about buying their coke in bulk from sellers who only sold higher quality more expensive coke behind closed doors, I was let out again in a place I had known for a large part of my life, the corner of Cambria Street. It was always nice to hang out with Wil, even if it was on the 2800 block of North Hancock Street. At the time, she was about seven months pregnant by my Cousin June, aka "Crazy Ace." Both of them were living at my aunt's house. When I was in Philly, this is the place I had become accustomed to spending my time because it was familiar. I had people there, and I was grateful to be permitted to visit sporadically.

When I walked inside the house, Wil and I embraced, relieved to experience kinship, if only for a limited time. We quickly caught up about each other's lives and went outside to sit on the front steps. She filled me in on who was dating whom, who was being used and abused by whom, who was having a baby, who was having an affair, who went to jail or the juvenile detention center, and who had gotten released.

In discussing the latest rumors, we talked about Juan Carlos and his determination to take back the corner we were sitting next to as soon as he had gotten out of prison. In this neighborhood, on any given day, drug dealers would inevitably get into some beef[38] and violence to eliminate threats to their livelihood was not uncommon.

We got hungry and walked over to the Chinese takeout place directly across the street from the corner we were chilling[39] on, less than ten feet away from a busy intersection that allegedly brought in over $3 million a year. We ordered some fried chicken wings and French fries to share. When the food was ready, we took it back across the street, went into the house, and ate it at the dining room table. After we finished our meal, we slowly headed toward the screen door with an unexplainable feeling about something being off. Before we had a chance to reach the handle, we noticed Juan Carlos directly across the street on the opposite corner in a parked car. A young girl was sitting next to him in the passenger seat talking.

Instinct warned us not to go back outside yet. Seconds later, an expressionless man rolled up onto Juan Carlos while he was still seated in the car. He stood over him with a .357 magnum and opened fire. We were speechless and unable to move as we watched Juan Carlos get shot in the head. His body fell to his right and onto the girl's lap. It wasn't the first crime we had seen growing up in the hood, but it was the goriest gangster-induced gunshot wound to the head the two of us ever witnessed within a few feet of us.

---

38 Argument
39 Hanging out

After the initial shock, we started to back away from the doorway, but not before seeing another man dart toward the vehicle, yank the girl out of the passenger seat, and throw her over his shoulder while she screamed in horror.

On this intersection and many others throughout the city, a guy standing on the corner selling illegal substances or getting into a drug dispute, was just part of the scene. It was all we had known and was nothing unusual. However, watching a trigger man pull out a gun and take another man's life reminded me of the real and present dangers of the environment.

I was fifteen years old and felt like I was in a real-life scene out of the movie "*Colors*," except Sean Penn, and Robert Duvall were nowhere around. As I watched a hitman fatally shoot and murder another human being on the corner of Hancock and Cambria, I was already aware of the snitches get stitches or worse philosophy. So, to say I looked forward to getting picked up was an understatement. If I wasn't around, I didn't have to worry about the cops trying to get a hold of me for a witness statement.

Wil and I only ever spoke of our familiarity with the details in private, never in front of anyone else. The last thing we wanted to do was give the cops a reason to drag us down to the police station. Some officials only put effort into trying to make their jobs easier and others' lives harder. Most members of the police department, in our experience there, harassed both criminals and those minding their own business. They did a lot of shady things and often risked the lives of innocent people.

Before the day turned into night, I had witnessed a murder that would make me question my uncertainty of how long I could live in Jersey with my boyfriend and his parents. I looked forward to getting on the Black Horse Pike or the Atlantic City Expressway.

On the ride back, I looked upon the farmlands we passed on the way to the townhouse. I realized that living in a place where everyone around me was snorting coke all the time wasn't so bad in comparison to where I could be living. I thought about how lucky I was and how I felt physically safer the closer we got to Mays Landing.

During the months I spent living in New Jersey, I wondered if, in spite of who I was living with, I could make it in an American suburb. Would I ever really be free from the Badlands? At what point, would I return to a life filled with young men who felt the need to defend their turf, taking it so far as to murder others to enforce their authority.

The fall of 1988 brought with it the bloodiest crime I had ever seen with my own two eyes. I was a reluctant witness who didn't want to describe the fatal shooting in a place where hurting people hurt people and occupants found it quite a challenge to minimize their exposure to a ravaged inner-city. Engaging in crime was almost always the only way for its young and old (if we lived that long), to secure funds, power, and status.

Chapter Eighteen
Breaking Nights

*"People have been having issues with substance abuse since the
dawn of time, I imagine, since they started fermenting fruit and
vegetables, for God's sake....I'll say that I don't think you can throw
a stone and not come in contact with someone who knows someone
or has problems with substance abuse." ~ Octavia Spencer*

I thought moving into a South Jersey townhouse would be a fresh
start for me outside the Badlands. I could leave behind the life
that tried to devour me from the day my grandmother went into
the ground. Instead, month after month, I felt increasingly
powerless to affect any change. And no matter how bad I wanted
to fit in, I was reminded at home, in school, and even in the local
mall that I did not belong.

My boyfriend's unwillingness to be the person I needed him to be
was rooted in the fact he had no intention of solving his white
powder problem, let alone recognize it existed. And if I weren't
careful, he would drag me down into the pit with him as he spiraled
out of control. He was not doing the occasional dime bags on the
weekends. His body and his parents, for that matter, built up such a
tolerance to the drug they had to inhale a progressively more
substantial amount of cocaine to feel an acceptable high.

By my sixteenth birthday, they were consuming "Eight Balls" in
one sitting. I don't recall a single thing about my birthday except for
my boyfriend wanting to spend the time with his parents getting high

— business as usual. In spite of my living with three other people, going to school, and working part-time, I felt isolated.

Nearly every weekend, their friends would drive over from Philly with two eight balls (quarter ounce), half ounces, or an ounce of coke. They were so preoccupied with drug use they withdrew from me. Three of them made snorting coke together a fun form of entertainment. It was a real family affair.

Near the end of my first detour into the burbs, my boyfriend and his parents picked up a batch of cocaine that was purer than what they were used to snorting. My boyfriend offered me some so I could stop complaining about what was happening in the house. I'd always say no because I was already naturally hyper. I didn't need a substance to raise the physiological activity in my body. If anything, I could use the opposite. I was very much the type of person who looked forward to closing my eyes and being able to sleep in the middle of the night. Rest was a nightly goal, and when attained, I was in heaven.

I sought calmness in my life because I was tired of the storms, the thunder leading up to them, and the lightning during thunderstorms. The pressure mounted so much I finally gave in, licked my finger and put it in the bag filled with a substance resembling baking soda more than granulated salt. I stuck the same dipped finger back in my mouth. The white powder tasted bitter and awful. It had an instant numbing effect, kind of like being at the dentist before they get started on a root canal or filling.

My boyfriend scooped a bit onto his fingernail and reached for my nostril. After I inhaled it, I felt a brain rush, which he could discern from my facial expression. With a rolled-up dollar bill in his hand, he asked if I wanted to try some more. I shook my head sideways and sat motionless on the edge of the bed. He teased me about doing a line of coke in a questioning manner, implying that it would make me chill for the rest of the night. "No," I replied softly. I spent the first few seconds wondering if a single hit could make my mind completely numb like it had my tongue.

Within minutes it was apparent one hit was too much for me. My heart began racing. I literally could not sit still. I wondered if my mother's mind went numb when she smoked crack cocaine and if that's why she didn't give me much thought. I wondered why my mom, my boyfriend, his parents, and "Tony Montana", the fictional character and main protagonist in the 1983 film "Scarface" were all so addicted to it. As I paced back and forth, entertaining the thought of dying, I hated the way it made me feel. The irony in it all.

The thing about cocaine and my body chemistry was they went together like oil and water. Instead of craving more, as lots of people shared was the case when trying coke, I made a huge deal about being scared I might have to go to the hospital. He was already too wired and made it a point to let me know he wasn't going to call his parents upstairs about my dilemma. He reassured me I would be fine and just needed some time to pass.

During the one-hit-wonder experiment, my blood pressure felt elevated. I walked around the bedroom in circles. I knew my boyfriend didn't want to involve his parents, but I was getting concerned and asked if we should go to the emergency room. "No!" he yelled before slamming the bedroom door. He was restless and went downstairs. He returned minutes later with a tall glass filled with cranberry juice and vodka. He demanded I drink it to make me stop panicking. I raised the glass to my mouth and gulped the entire drink down in 60 seconds. Minutes later, I expressed the need to urinate as well as difficulty self-calming. The look on his face let me know I was messing with his high. My head was still in a tailspin of hyperactivity. One hit was definitely too much of a stimulant for me.

His life revolved around cocaine. In between random jobs, it was either about getting a hold of his dealer or trying to find a place to do a dime bag, gram, or an ounce without me being around to object.

The story was starting to sound so familiar. I wanted to stop thinking and go to sleep.

There I was again, causing all kinds of drama by speaking up when things were not going well. I thought about the occasional weekend trips to and around malls in Mays Landing or down the shore to the beaches in Atlantic City, Wildwood, Sea Side Heights, and Ocean City. I wished I was at the beach with my toes swirling in the warm summer sand and the sun shining on my face. I imagined the sounds of the waves, thinking it was one of the only things I looked forward to when I departed the Badlands. After what felt like hours but was only minutes, I came down and fell asleep.

Several times a week, my boyfriend and his parents broke out the cocaine and broke night[40] while I slept. Like vampires, they would wake up when the sun was in the process of playing hide and seek with the sky. Then they got high and drank nonstop for 12-hour blocks of time without giving me a second thought. I saw it as a problem that was eroding and plaguing our relationship because each time this went on for hours until the blow[41] was all gone. They'd run out as the sun started to rise and the darkness would be eventually replaced with a brightness making its way through and to the other end of any visible line of sight. Like babies in need of feeding, they were cranky when their bodies craved another line.

When they were drinking alcohol and snorting cocaine at the same time, I could only wonder how dehydrated they were from the toxic combination and limited water intake. I preferred water to other drinks, as nothing ever really quenched my thirst like an ice-cold glass of water. Since they didn't drink much water, their hangover headaches were usually heightened and intensified with the slightest sound, like a microwave beeping when coming to a complete stop.

---

40 Stay up until the sun rose
41 Cocaine

Even between the distance of two floors, somehow after their cocaine binges, my boyfriend's mother developed superpower hearing which caused walking on the tile with the wrong pair of shoes to end in an angry outburst. If they managed to fall into a deep sleep, it would last well into the afternoon. Upon rising, they were the most irritable people in the world until the cycle started all over.

It was clear that my boyfriend's mother felt most superior and seemed to enjoy trying to make me feel like an inferior human she tolerated to keep her son within her reach. Although I was well aware of her barmaid-turned-seamstress-saved-by-the-local-lumberjack story (slight exaggeration about the lumberjack part), when she was coked-up, she often painted herself with grandiosity.

She appeared to possess the fixed mindset of women who enjoyed exposing the world to their narcissistic nature. She talked trash about my coming from a family of low-life drug users and didn't hesitate to degrade other people she knew back in Philly. Her pompous pretentiousness was so annoying I desperately wanted to move out. When she woke from her half-baked drug-induced slumber, she'd wake up her husband, if he wasn't already awake, and the two of them would demand that I do weird things like clipping his toenails, which I found disgusting. I'd always hesitate and take a brief moment of silence. I wondered what would happen if one day I screamed in response, "That's nasty; do it yourself!"

Before I finished whatever menial task these two conjured up for me, they'd mock me about the month I arrived in Mays Landing. Somehow, they thought it was hysterical how I kept walking up to one store manager after another, asking if they were hiring. I didn't understand why wanting to find a paying job when I moved in with them was funny. I sought employment opportunities for half my life.

At the age of nine, I tutored neighborhood kids. At eleven, I sold pretzels. At twelve, I got up in the middle of the night to pick blueberries in South Jersey blueberry fields during a distinct harvest window in the summer. There were thousands of acres of blueberries in Atlantic County, and although it was illegal, children my age were received in the Hammonton fields as we departed cramped buses without anyone seeming concerned about child-labor laws.

I earned about $2.50 per crate, and it took more than an hour to fill a single container, which meant I was getting paid much less per hour than minimum wage. It took all morning for me to fill two crates. By then, the sun was beaming on my back, making me sweat through my clothes. I ended up spending half my earnings on something to eat and drink for lunch. Considering the time and energy I expended, even at 12 it didn't take more than a handful of trips to figure out the return on the investment did not yield a positive return for me. At least I tried it out.

During the summers, I worked at a Chinese laundromat and the Philadelphia Anti-Graffiti Network. I had always been a worker who had no problem earning her keep or a little bit of money to live. Even though my mother got a government check, I didn't want a free ride from anyone. I was also determined to earn enough money to contribute to housing and food wherever I lived.

Chapter Nineteen
Break for Cover

"Our lives begin to end the day we become silent about things that matter." ~ Martin Luther King Jr.

Although no one was physically hurting me, forcing me to get high, or leaving me to starve, after returning home from school, I dreaded being in an environment where I was spoken down to, ignored, and mistreated. I frequently thought about a means of escape. Wil was still living with my aunt on Hancock and Cambria, so at the very least, I had to wait until she got her place. She was planning on it before her baby was born. In the meantime, I had to stay put because I had no place else to go. It meant my boyfriend could keep treating me like an afterthought and getting high to the point where he claimed to see and hear things I didn't.

It seemed the coke was not only causing him to sneeze blood-covered snot and shoot out particles of skin from his nostrils into his mother's bath towels, but it also caused him to hallucinate, even after the cocaine parties ended. I wondered how his parents were okay with him not being able to keep a steady job and showing signs of paranoia.

Once again, I was struggling to fit in at school. None of the girls showed any interest in connecting with me, and the one party I went to made it clear the guys were only interested in one thing. The predominantly white middle class I encountered at the mall was just another reminder that I did not belong.

I vividly recall minding my own business while making my way around the stores in the Hamilton Mall when I walked in the opposite direction of a well-dressed white woman who pursed her lips together while clinging tightly to her purse as she was about to pass me. As if it wasn't bad enough, she spoke a word in my direction. She looked dead in my face and said, "Scum!" right before entering a high-end department store.

I expected this type of response from crossing over the wrong side of Front Street in Philly, but I had no idea I would be treated this way when I moved to the burbs. I felt threatened by the world while simultaneously being made to feel like I was somehow a threat to it on the sole basis of my appearance. It's one thing to look away from my direction and pretend I didn't exist, but to call me scum in a hostile manner when I was there to spend some of my hard-earned tax dollars was just another indication that racism was alive and well in all parts of America.

Reasons for seeing the school counselor typically included college or career guidance, roster changes, concerns about a staff member, interest in a job, financial aid, poor grades, and a need to withdraw from school. If I showed up at the counselor's office Monday morning to talk through what I was going through at home or share my experience at the mall, I wondered if any of them would treat my concerns with any sense of urgency. Would I be told to get over it? Would I be placed in foster care? To what extent would my impatient nature and impulsiveness result in more symbolic detours through Pity Parkways, Badland Boulevards, and dead-end Cutthroat Cul-de-sacs?

Even if I had convinced my friend Wil to shelter me after she eventually moved into her place, what kind of future would I have? Neither one of us had any legitimate means of long-term sustainable support while residing in one of the highest crime-and-poverty stricken places in America. Fighting an ever-growing internal conflict, I repeatedly attempted to leverage my early childhood capacity for self-reflection and refusal to become a victim of circumstance. But it was freaking hard, I thought.

Then came another straw that broke my camel ass back. It was during the cold winter break. The day started with a trip to the mall. My boyfriend was taking me to Wilson's Leather to buy my Christmas gift. I picked out an expensive black leather skirt and a short matching jacket. I was excited to rock it with a red turtleneck I bought at another store on a separate trip. I didn't know where my mother and brother were during that holiday so I could wish them a Merry Christmas. No matter what, they were still my family.

I reached out to the only other person in the world who had treated me with nothing but love, even when we disagreed. Although I never had a sister in my life, she felt like one to me when I truly needed one. She looked out for me and apologized to others when I acted out because of reasons having nothing to do with the other person. It was as if I was related to her by blood —inside my heart, she truly felt like family. I picked up the house phone and called Wil to let her know I was going to be dropped off at her new place the next day to catch up and spend some time with her and her newborn, Julio. He was born on December 16, 1988.

A few hours later, I held Julio in my arms, and Wil took an instant picture of us with her Polaroid camera. Once the image was ready, she handed it to me, and in exchange, I gave her the baby. I stared into his tiny eyes and saw the sweetest soul with nothing but unconditional love staring back at me.

The blissful moment was rudely interrupted by my boyfriend knocking on the door, demanding that I get into the car because his parents went around the block and decided they did not want to come back to pick me up later. I had only been at Wil's house for a few minutes. I didn't want to leave. He insisted, so I hugged Wil, kissed the baby's cheek, and reluctantly got in the backseat of the sedan.

We made our way up to the 5th Street toward the bar that my boyfriend and his stepfather were always holed up in when they were in Philly. They parked the car; he left me with his mother and disappeared into the bar. His mother and I walked down the street about a half-block in the distance. We walked up to the steps, knocked on a raggedy looking door, and made our way into the living room, where I was instructed to have a seat on some plastic covered couches.

His 40-something-year-old mother went into the kitchen with an older lady that looked like she had lived a hard life. I could hear them gossiping and sniffing lines of coke in between random laughter.

My blood was boiling. It was Christmas Eve, and I was all dressed up sitting in some stranger's dark and dreary roach-infested house with nothing to do. It was North Philly in 1988 with no accessible distraction devices. I just sat there all alone in the darkly lit living room with no one to connect with while everyone around me got trashed.

I was disappointed that my boyfriend pawned me off on his mother. After fighting off one too many roaches trying to crawl up onto my lap and hang out with me, I had enough. I got up intending to get his mother's attention to let her know I was going to go outside to get some air. When I entered the room, she crunched up her eyebrows as if I was disrupting the vital task of her taking the next hit. I did not manage to get a single word out when the air twist of her hand dismissed me. Her body language made it evident she wanted me out of sight.

I stomped out of the room and went outside. Although I looked great, I was not warm enough to walk around too far without freezing. I walked over to the bar and peeked in the window. I didn't see my boyfriend anywhere inside and debated on whether I should go in, but I decided against desperately asking the bartender about his whereabouts.

As I made my way back to the roach-infested house where his mother was getting coked-up, it dawned on me that I traded in a crack head for coke heads. But not just any coke heads, a family of coke heads dominated by the matriarch of the crew who was a mean-spirited ungrateful woman that made me feel like I was living on Swindler Street. I felt tricked into a home filled with nothing but hardcore cocaine addicts just so her son could have someone to have sex with, which would keep him under her roof.

The only differentiation between this family and mine was money. I thought about the fact the stepfather was making over $85k a year and the mother about $15k, so together they brought in six figures of taxable income into the household. I knew because as much as this woman enjoyed putting me down, she had no issue getting me to do their taxes without paying me for my time and services. It was the only task I did for them which was not in the least bit degrading and brought me a real sense of accomplishment. Besides their utilities, mortgage and car payments, the majority of their money went towards funding their cocaine addiction.

I was too cold to remain outside without proper outerwear, so I went back into that roach-infested house. I marched into the kitchen and blurted out my desperate desire to be taken back to my friend Wil's house. I practically pleaded. His mother got up from her chair and walked toward me. She stood over me and screamed so loud in my face to get back on the couch my bangs parted to the side when greeted by the hot air of her heated breath. I didn't move an inch.

Her words conveyed how pissed she was about my repeated attempts to talk to her while she was in the middle of inhaling her coke. She brought up my crack head mother and my being lucky I wasn't living with her anymore. I told her my mother had nothing to do with this situation. Before I was able to get another word out, she raised her hand to my face and smacked me in a power play intended to shut me up and break my spirit. I remained where I was in shock.

I imagined myself yanking out her tight hair bun, holding her loose hair firmly with one hand, and swiftly catching her in the eye with my fist. In an alternate move, I envisioned raising one foot off the ground while holding both hands out to my sides and drop-kicking her dead in the face. But I wasn't Bruce Lee, and I wasn't the Karate Kid fighting to win a trophy after being beaten down by his ruthless opponent. Despite her coke habit, she was much heavier than I was with a huge gut. Nothing I did was going to cause her to drop to the ground. I could not believe slapping me was her final response to my reasonable request to be taken back to where I was peacefully chilling with my friend earlier in the evening.

My boyfriend and his stepfather happened to walk through the open front door. Both saw my grim facial expression. There were no words to explain how livid I was at that moment. Yet that didn't cause him to show grave concern toward me.

Needless to say, it was a long, cold, quiet ride back to Mays Landing. I had plenty of time to process what had just happened and plan my next move. On that ill-fated Philly night starting on Christmas Eve and ending early Christmas morning, I decided the abuse was over and liberation was in order.

As soon as we arrived, I dashed toward the house phone. As everyone else made their way upstairs before daylight, I hid in the first-floor bathroom and dialed Wil's number. The phone rang a few times before she answered. I asked if she was ready for me to move in and sleep on her couch until I figured out what to do after leaving the burbs. I whispered the story about my boyfriend's mother slapping me because I wanted to go back to her house. She said she could barely hear me, and we would talk more when I got to her home.

When I stepped out of the restroom; my boyfriend was standing right next to it, asking who I called. I told him I called Wil and wanted to go to bed. My boyfriend grabbed my hand and led me up into the bedroom where I had been sleeping with him since I left Philly. Once we got into the room, he tried to kiss me, but I turned my face away. He wanted to lead me to the bed, but I turned toward the closet to get a feel for how much stuff I had to pack up. He followed me into the closet and tried to lead me back out, but I was stocky and stood firm with my feet planted into the carpet. He gave me a bear hug and covered my five-foot 130-pound frame with his six-foot 250-pound body. My arms hung down on the side of my hips. He broke out in tears in the middle of the closet.

I whispered into his ear, "it's over". There was nothing he could say to convince me to stay there another night. His cry grew louder. I told him I didn't want to hear his mother's voice bitching at me anymore, her hands ever making their way to my face, or her physical presence anywhere near the air I was breathing. His grip on me grew tighter. His hug prolonged until I said what he did not want to hear departing from my mouth. I softly said, "I'm going back to Philly to live with Wil." I was grateful she agreed to shelter me.

I broke free from his grip and quietly crept into the shared bathroom next door while he remained in the closet sulking. I returned to the bedroom with a couple of plastic trash bags in hand, and he sprinted toward me. Within seconds, we were both seated on the edge of the bed, and he tried to pry the trash bags out of my hands. I refused to let go and started to fill one with clothes I was pulling out of the dresser drawers. I dumped my underwear and socks into a bag while he attempted to convince me to stay. I stopped listening. I blocked him out until I heard a noise in the shared bathroom next to the bedroom. I put everything down and laid down in the bed. He moved close to big-spoon me before he finally fell asleep.

The sunlight was shining in through the window blinds. I waited until my boyfriend was in a deep enough sleep to feel nothing when I moved his arm off me so I could slither off the side of the bed onto the floor. I contemplated my next move. I wanted nothing more than to finish packing up my stuff into the plastic bags so I could be ready for when his stepfather woke up. At the precise moment in time, nothing would have made me happier than to jet back to Philly.

If I had an alternate means of transportation, it would have happened the moment I walked into the front door. But I was stuck. Being entirely dependent on another person to help me move forward was one of the worst feelings in the world. I wanted to stomp down the stairs, out of the house, and into his stepfather's sedan to wait for a ride back to Philly.

Instead, on that cold Christmas morning, I tiptoed down the stairs of the 2-bedroom townhouse, moving slowly through the naturally lit hallway, cautious to remain unheard. I did not want to hear the wrath of the increasingly irritable matriarch who had only gone to bed moments earlier. I was still processing how a few short hours ago I had gotten slapped in the face for no justifiable reason. I knew if I stayed, my boyfriend's mother would continue to be fueled by a cocaine addiction which would only feed her desire to keep slapping me around whenever she wanted to make herself feel like a superior being. I headed toward the kitchen to satisfy my hunger. As I grabbed something to eat as quietly as I could, I wondered how none of the people sleeping upstairs had any feelings of shame about how they were living, or how they treated me.

Having spent most of my life with a drug addict, I was well aware that fighting an addiction, whether it was substance abuse or narcissism or both, required a person to admit their wrongs before reaching out for help. I wasn't going to keep allowing what I viewed as broken people to continue their attempts to break me. They all seem to be blind to the destruction of spirit taking place within their environment.

One thing was sure; I would not tolerate another moment where I would be verbally abused, treated like a toenail clipping slave, neglected, and slapped. I was startled by the sound of at least one person who was unable to sleep anymore. I went back upstairs and walked into a hallway disagreement at the top of the stairs between my boyfriend and his mother.

Since I was in the middle of all of it, I felt compelled to take an active role in the conversation. I expressed a great deal of disappointment by the disrespect shown. I said I tolerated a lot of crap and placing her hands on me was the last straw. In her twisted mind, she said I deserved it and informed me I had it good there, better than I would ever have it. She chastised me for wanting to go back to Philly. She said, "Go eat ground beef every day when you

119

could be having steak!"

Speaking Spanish, she instructed her husband to return me to the gutter promptly. I walked away and frantically searched for my measly belongings. Even though I found a way to escape my mother's regime and was residing in a newly built community in a safe municipality of Egg Harbor Township, it most certainly was not worth the tradeoff, I thought.

Physical residency at Wil's place on Palethorpe and Cambria Streets had to be better than the alternative life I was living with my boyfriend. It didn't matter if it was in a high-crime, low-income environment where the drug trade was the best shot most of its residents seemed to have at earning a livable wage. A place where more than half the youth dropped out of high school and spent most of their time on public assistance, shacked up with drug dealers and hustling on the streets to make ends meet. Before the sunset, I would be within fifteen minutes of the Badlands as soon as I saw exit 22.

Chapter Twenty
Breaking Me

"Out of anger comes controversy, out of controversy comes conversation, out of conversation comes action." ~ Tupac Shakur

My eyes stared at open fields of greenery and farmland for nearly 60 miles while my mind looked back on all the negative events of 1988. It was the year my mother took her crack use to a whole new level. The year the real risks of dropping out of Central High and losing my virginity had become a reality. The year I first witnessed a deadly gang shooting up close. The year I had to deal with the loss of dignity and respect from having ricocheted into suburban life and getting some of my Jersey Shore beach tan slapped off my face on Christmas Eve. It was the year I felt like my mother, my boyfriend, and his mother were testing my resilience as each took turns trying to break me.

By the time we got near the Delaware River, I was startled by the discussion regarding traffic and entering Philly through the Walt Whitman Bridge. Regardless of the route taken, it was a little over an hour's drive from Mays Landing to North Philadelphia, which I usually dreaded the closer we got to the Walt Whitman or Ben Franklin Bridges. But not this time. Did I have anxiety about what awaited me back in the City of Brotherly Love? I would have been lying if I said I did not. I was an at-risk youth trying to figure out how I was going to survive while my mother collected public assistance on my behalf.

I redirected my thoughts from the hostility I had encountered to the city. The further north we got into Philly, the more I felt like I was where I was supposed to be, under the circumstances. Soon, I would be back around the way and kicking it where the Tuff Crew got their fame, in "*My Part of Town*." At least I could listen to Power 99 F.M.'s "*The Street Beat*," which would fade from the radio by the time we were about 30 miles into Jersey.

I would be able to tune into and hear my favorite Philly DJ, Lady B. Through my teen years, I heard her play songs from the best rap artists at the time on her hip hop *Megamix*, which always made me forget about whatever was going on at home, at least while I was listening to the radio.

Evidence of Philadelphia's dense and highly populated Latino community showed itself as soon as we traveled into the commercial district on North 5th Street. I did not understand why it was called the Golden Block in Spanish because it was made up of more than a single block beyond the corner of 5th and Lehigh Avenue. The area reminded me of my first haircut, Spanish music, Latino art, and an authentic Puerto Rican food. The sounds coming from 464 Lehigh Avenue were like a magnet that drew people into Centro Musical, a Puerto Rican-owned music store. A place where "*Conga*" by Miami Sound Machine could be heard blocks away and made your hips shake the closer you got to the store entrance.

When there was an interest in unique original artwork, there was Taller Puertorriqueño. When I wanted to buy clothes or shoes, I went to Jerry's at the corner of 5th and Cambria where Jerry also sold ornamental Sweet Sixteen dresses and prom gowns, none of which I would ever buy. When the sales girls came over to wait on me, I would ask them to show me their casual wear, shoes, and accessories. To satisfy a craving for Spanish food, El Bohio at 2746 North 5th street was just a few footsteps away. The sidewalk painted with a wavy yellow strip in a tribute to the yellow brick road ended near Allegheny Avenue, a destination where I would never find Oz or magically become Dorothy.

By the time I arrived at Wil's house, *"Walk This Way"* by Run-D.M.C. was blasting in the background, and I was not dismayed. I thought to have a boyfriend like my cousin had just a couple of years earlier would have made me happier. Before I met him, I was depressed about my home environment, but I managed to pretend I was in Whitney Houston's *"I Wanna Dance With Somebody"* video.

Not long after we met, I was feeling the lyrics of Lisa Lisa and the Cult Jam's *"I Wonder If I Take You Home,"* followed closely by the girl group Expos' *"Point Of No Return."* When exiting the vehicle in front of Wil's house, I felt both relieved and hurt. My boyfriend hugged me tightly and said he would be back for me. I said, "Only if we live by ourselves." Before anything else came out of his mouth, I left him with words from Taylor Dayne's *"Prove Your Love"* and reminded him that until I saw evidence of it, we would not be listening to Al B. Sure's *"Nite And Day"* again.

I would resume listening to Power 99 F.M.'s Quiet Storm late-night radio soulful slow jams and contemporary R&B all by myself, just like I did before I let him into my life; at least it is what I told myself.

A roller coaster of highs and lows ensued, but it felt more like nonstop drama plunging into the unknown day after day. Before school resumed in January 1989, I connected with a woman who lived near Girard Avenue but worked at Oakcrest High School in South Jersey. She said if I could make it to her house by 6 a.m., she would give me a ride to school and back to Philly every day.

The first day I tried to make it in time, she left by the time I got to her house. I arrived out of breath after walking several miles south from Wil's house. I tried again and realized it was too dark, too early and it required too much effort. I didn't go to bed early enough, rise soon enough, or walk fast enough to make it before she left her house.

I applied for and got a job at Burger King, but after two days, I turned in my polyester uniform and did not bother returning to collect the $22 check.

I was starting to get even more depressed. I pondered how there was no going back to Central. That dream was dead, and there was no resurrecting it, I thought. So, I enrolled in the neighborhood zoned high school. I lasted only a month or two at Thomas Alva Edison High School located at 151 West Luzerne Street between 2nd and Front Streets in a new building within walking distance of Greenmount Cemetery. That cemetery was where grandmother and many others were buried after funerals filled with howling, sniffling, and elaborate memorial services and flowers placed around caskets.

Because of its outdated premises, Edison High School had moved from 8th and Lehigh on the east side of Germantown Avenue. The old school building and its castle-like exterior fitted with gargoyles who greeted its visitors had become an abandoned building. Drug users and vandals visited there when they wanted to explore what was inside to satisfy their curiosity. The vandalized structure, like tons of others throughout the city, was left behind as evidence of the post-industrialization era.

Old or New Edison, it was yet another high school I soon realized I didn't fit into either. I was a poor nerd with worn-down, acid-washed jeans I tried to chemically bleach myself. I could never quite pull off any trends of the time with any degree of confidence. When I tried to wear my short puffy tulle skirts over black leggings with cheap rubber bracelets and bleached wild hair as my only other accessory, I wasn't comfortable, and it showed. I had a few gold pieces my boyfriend bought me, but it wasn't enough to express the image of wealth valued in necks, arms, and fingers filled with shiny gold jewelry. Well-groomed popular teens pulling it all off lingered in hallways and outside during school hours. Some made out, some sold drugs, and others cut class to smoke weed blunts on the grass. I was never invited to partake in any of it.

With less than two full years of high school education, I transitioned my thoughts to fast-tracking my path to profitable employment. I told myself that I would not lose sight of one day going to college. I told myself I was going to pursue a different route.

After dropping out of Central, Oakcrest, and Edison, I discovered a school that could be a realistic alternative. Attending business school meant I would never go to prom, graduate or be eligible to apply to LaSalle or Temple University or so I thought. I wondered what kind of lives my old Central peers would be living after graduating from one of these schools or an expensive private Ivy League institution of higher education like Wharton, where many said they would go after graduation.

Given my situation, I took out a student loan of approximately $5,000 and enrolled in Watterson School of Business and Technology. My intention was to obtain a Word Processing Specialist Certificate I could use to secure a decent job in business using computers. I caught SEPTA to the school at 5800 North Marvine Street. My new plan was to take advantage of the training for an entry-level profession. The school administrators claimed to help students get jobs performing word processing after obtaining certificates.

Watterson also had a security guard program. I found my mother and convinced her to enroll in that program. Amazingly enough, she did. However, within several weeks she dropped out.

In the meantime, I missed my boyfriend. When we argued over the phone, I would go up into Steven's bedroom and ball up in a fetal position on his tiny twin bed. When Wil called up and asked if I was okay, I tried to hide the sounds of my pain through a one-word response, "Yes". Strangely, my heart literally felt like someone was holding it in their hands and crushing it, something I had never experienced. When he came to Philly to visit, the physical pressure I felt in my heart disappeared. He'd bring me more gold jewelry and gassed me up[42] with delusions of grandeur. It didn't take much before I jumped in the sedan and got dropped off with him in front of the Days Inn on Roosevelt Blvd. I believed most things my boyfriend told me and mistook his words and affection for this thing called real love.

By the time spring leaves were bursting forth from the trees, I had missed my period and was wondering if the next scheduled period would show up. It never did. Days later, I found out I was pregnant. I had to come up with a new plan to escape the streets of Philadelphia, gain valuable employment skills, obtain my high school equivalency diploma, and secure an office job.

Even though the program at Watterson was scheduled to end after I was due to deliver, I decided I would continue to attend classes as long as I could before giving birth. I convinced my boyfriend to get us a place of our own. So, he convinced his parents to rent us the house they used to live in on the 2800 block of Lee Street.

As soon as he got comfortable, he went back to his usual routine of working inconsistent construction jobs and getting high daily. I started to sell Avon around Lee Street between Cambria and Somerset Streets. I knew his drug addiction was getting bad again when I came home after collecting cash from a prior sale to add a few more dollars to the two hundred-dollar stash I had hidden under my mattress. I was utterly shocked when I uncovered the money was gone, and so was my boyfriend. When I asked around for him, someone said he went to Wildwood for the weekend. I could not believe he stole my Avon money and left me alone while I was five months pregnant.

---

42 Told me whatever he thought I wanted to hear

By that point, my mother was living in a run-down house a couple of houses down the street from Wil's row home, so I moved in with her, thinking we could make it work this time. She had finally moved from Randolph, which was a couple of blocks to the east of North Marshall Street where Gary Heidnik had lived and was caught victimizing vulnerable neighbors. Buffalo Bill, in the movie "Silence of the Lamb," was the character modeled after this certifiably mental man who kidnapped, imprisoned, raped and assaulted women.

Due to the missing cash incident, I stopped selling Avon and asked my aunt Angela, who moved back from Rhode Island if I could work at her hair salon on the corner of Palethorpe and Cambria. I was visibly pregnant. I couldn't go job hunting anywhere else. She was a licensed cosmetologist who agreed to pay me to wash hair and sweep floors. It wasn't much, but it was enough to buy Chinese takeout down the street on the corner of Hancock and Cambria. It was either that or meals made from the ingredients allowed as part of the Special Supplemental Nutrition Program for Women, Infants and Children (W.I.C.). A program created to help low-income pregnant, breastfeeding, and non-breastfeeding postpartum women and infants and children up to age five who are found to be at nutritional risk.

I wasn't at my mother's place long when I saw a fat black rat almost the length of a ruler scurry through the room in broad daylight. I didn't want to go back to my boyfriend's house on Lee Street, and even if I did, his parents had enough of our drama. I was desperate again, so while he was trying to convince me to forgive him, I convinced him to rent out a place not tied to his parents. He found an apartment pretty quickly. When I returned to my mother's house to pack up my stuff, I discovered she had stolen all my gold jewelry and the microwave I bought before moving in.

I found someone on the block who still had a couple of my gold rings left before they resold them. One was a gift from my boyfriend, and the other was a lion head with a ruby. I bought the lion head for my mother because she was a Leo and loved lions. Not smart if your mom is a crack head. I repurchased both rings and considered the rest a loss.

Shortly thereafter, I found my mother near a stash house I was hoping she wasn't planning to raid. There was no point in scolding a grown woman with sunken eyes and a drawn face who didn't have the slightest interest in hearing anything not contributing to her next fix.

My boyfriend and I ended up moving to an apartment near the corner of 5th and Wyoming next to a bar and behind a check-cashing business. The place had a small bedroom, tiny kitchen, and a bathroom not big enough to fit more than two people. You could not fit more than a handful of people in all its combined rooms. He said he would get us a better place before the baby was born and puffed out his chest as if that would make his words more believable.

However, as I entered my third trimester, there was no indication he was trying to do anything other than support his coke habit. Most of my nourishment came from W.I.C. cereal, which I often ate for breakfast, lunch, and dinner. I loved my family because they were all that I had, but none of them reached out to see how I was doing. And I didn't contact Wil because I didn't want her to know how bad things had gotten since I left the block.

As my belly grew, so did my anxiety about a life surrounded by addicts. There were too many lonely nights where I cried myself to sleep in that 5th Street apartment. I rarely saw my boyfriend, and when I did, he looked gaunt and ghostly. He would never stay around for too long. I was so emotional, not a day went by when I didn't randomly burst into tears.

For me, worrying became a mainstay. One day, toward the end of summer, he barged in through the side window of the apartment, with his friends outside, shouting, "Blitz, get the gat!" Like a full-fledged gang member who took one too many coke hits that day, he didn't even acknowledge my presence. He frantically searched for a weapon I had no idea he had hidden in our apartment. As soon as he found the sawed-off shotgun he was seeking, he disappeared like a Ninja, as quickly as he arrived. I heard voices telling him they were all strapped and ready to bust a cap in that G's ass. It sounded like he was up to no good in the hood while I awaited the arrival of our unborn offspring alone night after night.

I needed a scene change, so I took SEPTA downtown toward City Hall. I walked in front of a poster that featured Mary Elizabeth Mastrantonio's name on it, and I recalled her as the sister in "Scarface." I liked her curly hair. In all her movies, she made it look manageable to maintain without the excessive frizz factor I had to deal with on a hit-and-miss basis. The film she was playing in was about a team searching for a lost nuclear submarine who encountered danger on their journey into the abyss when they found themselves face to face with an alien aquatic species.

I walked over to the movie theater ticket booth and said, "One for *'The Abyss,'* please." It felt strange to say one. Who went to the movies alone, let alone when visibly pregnant? People who felt like I was feeling; that's who. I could use some science fiction fantasy, given the harsh reality I was living. It felt weird walking into the theater alone and sitting there, staring at the screen, with no one to comment to about this excursion at the bottom of the Atlantic Ocean.

Over two hours later, I found myself wishing there was a search-and-rescue mission for me. I wasn't a sunken nuclear submarine, but I had sunken to an all-new low. I had to figure out how to keep hope alive and hang on to the belief things would eventually get better.

On a brisk early fall day, I arrived back to the 5th street apartment from an O.B. visit, wondering why there was a padlock on the entry gate. I asked myself what the hell was going on and why I heard 2

Live Crew songs from *"As Nasty As They Wanna Be"* blasting through the doors and windows. The music was so loud, yelling was useless. I had to think of a solution to solve my apartment entry problem. I walked back out the alley toward Wyoming and went inside the restaurant next to the bar on the corner. I asked a man who looked like he was in charge of the place if I could borrow a hammer because I could not get into my home. He looked down at my belly and asked if I needed any help.

I said, "No, thanks; I got this ... just need a hammer for a few minutes." He reached under the counter and came around in my direction to hand me the hammer.

Within two minutes, I was standing in front of the gate lock, slamming it as hard as I could until it finally broke off in pieces that scattered all over the concrete. I stepped over the remnants of the lock and up the apartment steps. I turned the key, pushed the door open, and found my boyfriend engaging in an early afternoon party with some of his homeboys and girls who either dropped out or were cutting school to get drunk and high with him at our place. I could barely breathe without inhaling some of the weed that was still permeating throughout the air.

I lost it, unplugged the source of the music from the wall, and started hollering, asking questions I knew the answers to and demanding everyone get the fuck out. After they left, I threw our wicker-backed dining chairs and glass table across the kitchen floor in a rage. I asked my boyfriend how he could find time to party but not make going with me to my O.B. doctor visits a priority. Right before he darted out the back door, he hollered, "I don't wanna fight!"

I sat on the kitchen floor, crying and wondering why I ever trusted what he said to me before I dropped out of Central. Why did I ever go with him in the first place? More importantly, why did I go back to him after leaving Mays Landing?

Chapter Twenty-One
Break of Dawn

"What kept me sane was knowing that things would change, and it was a question of keeping myself together until they did." ~ Nina Simone

On Friday, September 29, 1989, I caught a bus south, then another headed east toward the Episcopal Hospital in time for an early morning appointment. When I arrived, they did the usual poking and prodding. I thought I would be back on the bus by early afternoon because I wasn't due for another month or two. Instead, the O.B. admitted me into an inpatient room. When the nurse asked if I needed anything before her shift ended, I asked for the remote. I wanted to watch ABC's new TGIF line up of family-friendly comedies which now included one of my favorites, "Full House."

I woke up at the break of dawn listening to the chatter of a doctor telling a nurse they were going to induce me. Up to that point, I didn't feel a thing. As soon as they broke my water, I felt the most excruciating pain I had ever felt in my entire life. It was so bad I could not even describe it in a way that conveyed the extent of what I was feeling.

The chronic area-specific discomfort in my lower back was so severe, I moved the bed while still in it toward the hospital room door. A nurse pushed me back into the spot designated for the bed. The extreme lower back pain made me wonder if the baby was coming out of my butt. My agony worsened by the hour.

I repeatedly told myself I would not get pregnant again. At some point, I must have said those words out loud because a nurse appeared in my room and said, "All you teenagers in this neighborhood say that, and then you come back here year after year to have one after another!"

I thought her words lacked a bit of sympathy, considering my condition and the fact that she was a nurse. She was blond, pale, and visibly Caucasian, yet her last name was Lopez. It made me wonder if she was married to a man with a Spanish surname.

The hospital staff walked in and surrounded my hospital bed. They updated each other and said, "the patient is fully dilated." The baby's head was pressing down in preparation for fetal descent. The passageway was ready for me to push the baby from my uterus down through the birth canal to delivery. I demanded pain relief.

Even though an epidural was the most popular form of relief during childbirth, the nurse said it wasn't my decision to make. The doctor indicated I had to go through labor without any medication. I started begging and asked, "Why not?" An epidural wouldn't be approved because of my blood work, they said. There was concern about my blood pressure, and the placement of an epidural was just too risky. I was instructed to start pushing.

The pushing stage was complicated. I would put all my effort into pushing as hard as I could, and the baby's head would begin to emerge. I would get excited about the possibility of being done with this exhausting but game-changing task. Then I'd stopped to catch my breath, and all my efforts seemed wasted. The head would slip back into my vagina as if there was a game of peek-a-boo taking place in the hospital room. If I was going to get this task right on the next try, I had to conserve my energy and rest up for the next round of intense, uninterrupted pushing.

After six hours of suffering and countless rounds of stop-and-go pushing, I finally regained enough strength for one final push to get the nice-sized head out. The shoulders followed a bit more easily in comparison to the effort it took to get the head to fully emerge. The entire experience changed my world.

On September 30, 1989, at about 3 p.m., after the hardest I had ever worked in my life, I gave birth to my first baby blessing, who weighed in short of six pounds. I would not turn seventeen for another eleven days, but when they cleaned up his bloody body and placed him on my chest, it was time to act like an adult. I fell in love with him instantly, and the light in his eyes was like looking into heaven — a place I had never seen on this earth.

I went through various emotions. They explained the root cause of the yellow coloring in his skin and eyes. It occurred when a baby had a high level of bilirubin in the blood, which was a yellow substance the body creates when it replaces old red blood cells. They said he would be placed under lights because he had jaundice. I understood newborn jaundice was common.

After those initial few minutes of pure joy, they took him away, and I immediately doze off to Michael Jackson's *"Man in the Mirror"* playing inside my head: "... I'm going to make a change For once in my life. It's gonna feel real good. Gonna make a difference, gonna make it right ..."

When I woke up and asked for my baby, a brief thought about where his father was entered my mind. As they handed the baby to me, I redirected my focus. I looked at my newborn infant's face in awe. I was amazed by the beautiful life I created. He was mine to look after, to watch as he grew up, and to love with all my heart.

The birth of my son would be a catalyst for my mother's first breakthrough. It was the reason she finally made an effort to move in the direction of recovery. She managed to take a break from alcohol and drugs to come to see him at the hospital. She was so happy he was a boy; it was easier to negotiate with her about going to rehab. Actually, it was more of an ultimatum. I said if she didn't stop doing drugs, she could not be around my baby boy.

Through all her failures and missteps, she told me being around him was the one thing worth giving up drugs for, go figure. The arrival of my son drove her to seek treatment for years of chronic substance abuse. The road would never be bump-free for any of us, but this one decision resulted in her spending the rest of her life under psychiatric care with counselors who would prescribe medications and, lifelong behavioral therapy.

It was time for me to get emancipated. I plotted the steps I would take to remove my name as a dependent on my mother's blue Department of Public Welfare medical services eligibility card. Emancipation was a legal mechanism by which a minor was released from control by their parents or guardians, and the parents or guardians freed from responsibility toward the child.

In my mother's case, the latter didn't matter much since we were well beyond her having control or responsibility for me. Becoming an emancipated minor meant I could apply for public assistance on my own to obtain food stamps for myself and my son while I found a way to break the cycle of poverty.

During our hospital stay, my baby slept most of the day. He woke up to get a diaper change after taking a bottle. As a formula-fed baby, he woke up every 2-3 hours and seemed satiated at the end of a feeding. He was early from a gestation perspective, but his jaundice had cleared up within 72 hours. His physical exam and tests indicated he was ready to go home.

I was told I should expect to bleed for almost a month, with the possibility of spotting after, and at no time was I to put anything

inside my vagina. No problem. It was the last thing on my mind.
Sometimes the blood flow was even, and other times, it came out
intermittently in gushes. If I was lying down for a while, and blood
accumulated, I'd see some small clots in the toilet bowl. Fortunately,
it was my understanding that none of it was anything to be
concerned about, as it was all normal after childbirth.

I only needed a couple of stitches since there was no tear in need
of significant repairs. They said, it would take some time to recover
and feel like my old pre-pregnancy self again. While I was okay with
the recovery part, I didn't want to feel like my old self anymore.
Aside from the weight of the baby and placenta, I lost more weight
from the amniotic fluid the days after delivery and wanted to rid
myself of feeling like a victim. The guidance I needed on how to
feed the baby, keep him safe in the crib and the importance of well-
child check-ups was provided before I was discharged.

When we got back to the 5th street apartment, a white wicker
bassinet was waiting for us. After I took care of diaper changes and
feedings, I laid my precious baby boy in the bed next to me and
spent hours admiring his face as well as touching his tiny hands and
feet.

During the day, I made phone calls about getting emancipated
and figuring out what was needed to finish my program and receive
my Watterson School of Business and Technology Word Processing
Specialist Certificate so I could get a job. Unfortunately, my baby's
daddy continued his routine even though we had a child to raise.

Not long after, when the baby and I returned to the 5th Street
apartment after a pediatric check-up I found a fat scary-looking rat
inside the baby's bassinet. It looked like it was related to the one I
saw at my mother's house earlier in the year. I could not stay there
another night. I beeped my baby daddy 911, and when he called me,
I told him about the danger of having a rat crawl on the baby. I
convinced him we had to move. In turn, he convinced a friend of his

to let the three of us stay in one of their empty three bedrooms off the corner of 5th and Cayuga, near the bar he frequented often.

The baby and I didn't stay there long. I grew tired of him giving me a few bucks and then asking for it back and then some so he could disappear. Luckily, my mother had been clean for a few months, and her girlfriend told me that I could come to stay with them at her place on the 3700 block of Randolph Street. She had an extra empty bedroom, and the two of them could help provide a support system while I finished up my last Watterson classes and searched for work.

I found myself at Wil's house more often, and we bonded as spectators to a multitude of crimes in an environment we had no choice but to remain in as we grew closer daily. When we hung out, people started to ask us if we were sisters, which I thought was interesting because I was five-foot-tall and more olive-skinned, and she was five-foot eight and fair-skinned. I had curly hair, and she had straight hair. Her dad was Puerto Rican, and her mom was white. Her mom's genes were the dominate ones, giving her predominately Caucasian features like her skin color, hair texture as and finely pointed nose. She did inherit her dad's Puerto Rican eyes, which were similar to mine in shape and probably the reason why people asked if we were sisters.

On February 15, 1990, I got my Watterson School of Business and Technology Word Processing Specialist Certificate.

I was finally holding my certificate. However, the employment leads that the school sold us on during the enrollment process were nonexistent.

On February 27, 1990, my boyfriend signed a document titled Court of Common Pleas of Philadelphia County, Acknowledgment of Paternity and Waiver of Trial. I was still collecting welfare, and it was a government requirement so they could go after the fathers of children fed by public assistance.

Besides the shape and brown color of our eyes, the one thing Wil and I both grew to have in common was a deep disdain of poverty. Wil and I were always in search of work and ending up asking John

Ko, a sporting goods chain store owner if he would hire us at Olympia Sports. Mr. Ko, as his employees would all call him, placed Wil in the front of the store to sell sportswear, sneakers, shoes, and boots.

In 1990, while Wil used her good looks and charm to make money selling, I used all I learned in business school to keep track of the well-known retailer's inventory for the fashion-conscious neighborhood patrons on his computers. I was put in the back to manage inventory and bookkeeping. I tracked a wide range of athletic footwear and apparel coming in and out of the store, along with the corresponding pricing. On lunch break, we would go next door to Four Sons Pizza on the corner of Front and Dauphin Streets across SEPTA's York-Dauphin Station and tear into some pizza.

Mr. Ko also had a store at 2732-34 Germantown Avenue near 11th Street and Cumberland Streets in my old Hartranft neighborhood and another in West Philly at 5212 Market St near the 52nd Street SEPTA Station. I was sent to the one in West Philly a few times when they were shorthanded. It was the same type of environment, except the area population was predominantly African American on the West Side of Philly.

I had a great deal of respect for Mr. Ko. He was a successful businessman in his thirties who was not only the owner of a string of Philadelphia sporting goods stores, but he was also a Korean immigrant who wanted a better life and was willing to give two teenage girls in the hood a chance to make a better life too. It wasn't much, but those few dollars he paid us under the table helped when welfare checks just weren't enough.

Making it work was a challenge in more ways than one. In the spring of 1990, I was standing at the bus stop at the corner of Randolph and Butler, about three blocks from 8th and Butler, which was considered the city's most notorious drug corner. Like a bolt of lightning, a crack addict wearing a do-rag came out of nowhere, slammed her hand on my chest, snatched off the gold cross chain I was wearing, and ran off before I had a chance to look down at my neck. The bus was coming down the street, but I walked back home in complete disbelief over what just happened.

My mother and her friend were watching my baby, and I heard her friend call him "Cabby" as I walked in the front door. She called him that because she said he looked like a Cabbage Patch Kid with his round head and chubby cheeks. I walked past the baby and my mother's friend as I made my way up the stairs. My mother called out "China?" from the bedroom and inquired about why I was back so soon. I went into the bedroom and told her I just got mugged.

My heart was pounding. She asked me if I fought back, and I said I didn't get a chance. I wanted to cry to release the pressure. My mother had her issues, but she never took shit from anyone.

There must have been something going on with the moon because right after I got mugged, I was sitting on the steps in front of the house on the 3700 block of Randolph when a handful of girls approached me. I didn't look away from any of them, which prompted one to ask, "What the fuck are you looking at?" Without waiting for my response, they decided it was a good day to jump me.

I tried to fight them off. I even took out my frustrations on at least one of them before my mother heard the noise outside and came to the front door to investigate. When she stopped doing crack, my mother gained a significant amount of weight. But it didn't slow her down when she saw what was going down. Like a heavyweight Samurai wearing a sleeveless shirt and cut-off denim shorts, she moved swiftly in my direction. When the girls saw my mother approaching them, they darted down the block toward Erie Avenue. It was clear they didn't want to feel the wrath of Billy Boy.

The next day, my mother's friend decided she wanted to update her album pictures before I took my son to the zoo. I didn't have any

139

marks on my face from the mugging or getting jumped; so, I readied myself and the baby. I blow dried my bangs, put on my bamboo gold earrings, and laid on the thick eyeliner. I went down to the basement where my mother was doing laundry.

Her friend took a picture of the baby after I sat him in a tiny wicker chair next to the kerosene heater, which didn't have any fuel in it.

Wil and I were out of work. We consoled ourselves by going clubbing. I was seventeen but it didn't matter. It was pretty easy to get a fake ID. After random nights of drinking and dancing at places like Sylvie's, we'd head over to Aramingo Diner in Port Richmond or get up for an early morning breakfast at Olympia Restaurant at 127 West Allegheny Avenue, on the corner of Howard Street.

A few months later, my abilities were still out of alignment with legit work opportunities. To supplement a minuscule welfare check of about $300 a month I had to do something. It wasn't enough to cover expenses, food, clothes, toiletries, baby formula, and diapers. In my mind, I rationalized reaching out to a caseworker on Hancock and Cambria. I questioned selling drugs on the corner or standing on the corner and watching out for the cops. The latter was a lower risk but also a much smaller reward.

Once I got on the block, I moved forward with my decision to sell a bundle of dime bags. Before I even sold the first bag, I could not stop looking over my shoulder and worrying about getting robbed or busted by an undercover narc. I thought about the best and worst-case scenarios. Would I end up being dragged to the railroad tracks and left for dead? Somewhat drastic, but I recalled once when I decided to take a short cut during my inner-city travels; I almost got caught by someone following me into the "The Tracks" mini corridor where bodies lay hidden.

The mile-long wooded stretch of shipping railway cutting cross Lehigh and Allegheny Avenues was an area I stayed away from ever since my intuition caused me to look back and see what looked like a crazed stranger gaining on me.

When most people got shot or died, a new mural would go up within days. Would I get a painting with my face and name if I got killed on the corner? Aside from being killed, the worst-case scenario would be getting caught. Not only would a conviction record hinder my future opportunities for legit career advancement, I could lose my son.

Best case scenario, I sold my bundle and went on my merry way. Second best-case scenario, a crooked cop would shake me down, take my money and drugs for personal use, and let me go with a firm scolding. I thought about what I would do if there were signs of danger. I could throw the drugs down the sewer, behind a car tire, or in an abandoned house before running inside the Chinese take-out restaurant on the corner. As I paced back and forth near the of corner on Hancock and Cambria Streets, I wondered whether the reward outweighed the consequences of new issues I would have to deal with due to the risks I was taking. I thought, **what if something happened to me? Who was going to take care of my son**?

My mother was finally in recovery. **If I didn't stop what I was doing, there was an extremely high probability of it leading to a downward plunge into irreparable outcomes**. If the risk of my going to jail turned into a reality, I had to deal with the issue of Child Protective Services or the Department of Human Services, placing my son in foster care. Technically, I was still a juvenile; so, if I got caught, it was more likely we would both be placed in foster care.

I wanted my son to grow up to be proud of me. How could I teach him right if I was doing something so wrong? I wondered at what point did I decide to engage in a life of crime. What short-sightedness on my part to take on the "whatever happens, happens" philosophy. I didn't want to be this type of person. I refocused my thoughts on the life I wanted to live.

My baby boy's first birthday would arrive days before my eighteenth birthday when in the eyes of the law, I would be seen and treated as an adult. It was my responsibility to love him and care for him but also teach him right. How was I ever going to do that if I was dead or locked up? My baby deserved better.

All these thoughts instilled a desire to get rid of the remaining dime bags in my bundle. I wanted to take my cash cut and hand the rest of the money to the caseworker in return for the drugs he trusted me to sell. My son was about to turn one. How would he spend his first birthday? What would I do to acknowledge his birth? The decision I made could lead to a brighter future with more opportunities to thrive than threats to survival.

To give him a fighting chance, I had to become a productive contributing tax-paying member of society. I wondered **how I could I get from where I was to where I wanted to be.**

142

Chapter Twenty-Two
Breaking Free from Fear

"I have learned over the years that when one's mind is made up, this diminishes fear; knowing what must be done does away with fear." ~ Rosa Parks

I thought about the day I saw my mother smoke crack out of a Coke can without her having the slightest idea the incident would incite the formation of a fork in the road within my mind. A road I reached after an early plateau in my freshman year of high school. One where the path I chose led to radical life changes.

When I looked into the face of the adorable innocent smiling child I gave birth to months earlier, I knew even though I wasn't an adult yet, I was fortunate I had not gotten arrested or convicted of any crimes. I didn't want my son to experience "the malicious underbelly of urban life" in a world that had almost devoured me.

I was born into a world of hustling to survive and thrive, but there had to be an escape for both of us beyond the treacherous journey which had been my life's story. I realized many of my own decisions contributed to the reality I was living. I was nearing another turning point where a new road to a better life was on the horizon.

It was time to discontinue blaming people and circumstances. It was time to stop telling myself lies. It was time to stop making excuses. Even though I could not control what was happening around me, I could exercise greater control over my thoughts and the decisions I made from that point forward. If history taught me anything, it was I had to remove myself from a path which left me exposed to feelings of guilt, unworthiness and shame.

As I looked back on my own missteps, it became crystal clear that if I wanted things to change, I had to look in the mirror and make a change in me, just like the Michael Jackson song lyrics. I had to recognize it was my responsibility to make change happen. I decided to stop the direct exposure to occupational hazards and become much more risk-adverse. I could no longer keep operating under the assumption things were the way they were, and any real effort on my part would be fruitless. I would have to stop abandoning thoughts of putting forth enough effort and make moves to affect and change the status quo.

If the definition of insanity is doing the same thing over and over and expecting a different result, I had to realize life was not going to magically get better unless I did something different. If I was going to learn from my mistakes, I had to learn that anything good and worth having was going to take time and sacrifice to acquire. I had to accept that when things felt painful, I had to be out of alignment. I realized if I stopped putting in enough effort or quit too soon, my situation might never change, or it could get worse like it did after I dropped out of Central High School.

I thought about my first concert just a couple of weeks earlier. It was Janet Jackson's Rhythm Nation 1814 World Tour, which was at the Spectrum Arena for the sold-out show that took place in August. Protest songs were made famous by soundtracks such as the one associated with Spike Lee's "Do the Right Thing." It was rare in my neighborhood to find someone who would not bob their head in agreement with the likes of Public Enemy in their iconic "Fight the Power." Political statements to this degree were rare in R&B.

Janet Jackson took a page out of Public Enemy's book and included social and political topics in song lyrics like "State of the

World," which I could relate to in my everyday life. I watched her entertain the audience with intricate choreography in sync with her singing and costume changes. The expensive ticket was a gift to me, and I wanted to buy my concert tickets in the future without having to sell a bundle of dime bags or owe anyone anything.

I arrived at another fork in the road. But this time, my son was looking up at me from his stroller, dependent on me to make decisions and take action leading us to an alternative reality.

His face and an inner voice motivated me to become the architect of our new future and envision a different world than the one we were living in within the Badlands. I visualized myself growing in my field of interest and helping others understand how my passions could help achieve goals, eventually lead me to a fulfilling management career taking me outside of my current environment. I had to accept that I was entirely responsible for my receptivity. My ability and willingness to take in information or ideas was up to me and I had to stop making conditions over things I could not control. I asked for a new reality. I had to allow myself to see it and feel it before it came to be because I was the creator of my future. I had to tune into the frequency of who I was, at my core.

I saw what drug caseworkers did with tasks such as planning resources across all shifts and ensuring timely execution of required work within the 24 x 7 business. I felt I could do that someday in a legitimate setting. I imagined being like the Puerto Rican version of the Melanie Griffith character in "Working Girl." I started to paint a mental image of myself in a chic boardroom suit, working my way up the ladder within business.

I made up my mind to stop the pity party and start a new journey toward self-improvement. I began to view effort as a path to mastery. I thought about the curiosity I had abandoned. Creating a legitimate working girl vision filled me with a definite sense of resolve. I held firmly onto my foundation and onto hope about the possibilities for the future. I thought, what I should be doing next to get to that new destination?

The answer that came to me was to make it my mission to build on my strengths and develop my skills. I could make the most of my potential in an administrative position I enjoyed with opportunities for growth where I could contribute while having my efforts appreciated. I could see myself as that ambitious secretary who took off her sneakers while seated in the office chair. I painted a picture of myself putting on a pair of black high-heeled shoes and shifting into a growth mindset that would position me to take action as I climbed the business ladder to success. I was starting to get excited about the possibility of moving from the corner to a cubicle.

After I refined the image in my mind of what my future would look like in an ideal state and the work I would do as part of my new mission, I wondered, how do I make both a reality? An inner voice prompted me to examine myself and my surroundings in the context of what I wanted to do and see. I mentally explored, identified, and analyzed myself and my environment in terms of what was favorable and what was not. In doing so, it became blatantly apparent that eliminating the threats of continuing to seek supplemental income on a treacherous corner was non-negotiable. I completed an analysis of my internal strengths after thinking about the achievements I was most proud of as far as my abilities, skills, education, certifications, and connections. I came up with the following:

- Reliable employee
- Able to follow instructions and request clarity, if needed
- Capable of completing assignments fully and on time
- Proficient in the use of computers and Word Processing

I gave thought to what values differentiated me from others, and I felt that the main one was integrity. Lying was not something I was comfortable with, and I believed all people to be equal, which guided me to embrace, respect, and treat everyone equally while expecting the same from others.

I pondered my weaknesses and evaluated where I had a deficiency in skills, training, and education. My negative work habits and personality traits included the following:

- Honest and direct in communication; blunt with words
- Tendency to avoid recovering from setbacks

If I had to identify external threats and obstacles slowing down or affecting progress:

- Being born into poverty on an unleveled playing field
- Lack of safe housing and constant displacement
- Lack of family assistance or partner support

I listed how the environment could negatively impact us:

- Amplification of the "War on Drugs"
- City police known for being a "petri dish for corruption" (quote by The Philadelphia Inquirer)
- By September 9, 1990, the Philadelphia Police Department reported 337 homicides
  - Most killings were a Black or Hispanic victim in incidents involving drug motives and gunshots

Opportunities in trends affecting business and growth:

- According to the U.S. Bureau of Labor Statistics, women in the labor force was up (more specifically, increasing from 41% in 1967)
- U.S. economic data studies predicted an extensive demographic transformation in the labor force diversifying as people of color and "minorities" entered into it
  - Coupled with the arrival of women, these workforce factors played a part in growing the economy.
- Business document preparation by way of written reports on yellow legal pads and manual or electric typewriters replaced with "Wang" standalone word processing systems. Software I was skilled in using based on what I learned in business school. I could leverage my understanding of technology to establish a career and advance my mission.

The outcome of my assessment helped me focus on redirecting my thoughts and energy into finding a way to break into the business. I also looked at how connections might help me advance my mission.

While I did not have family members, friends, or associates that could make introductions in business, I enjoyed reading about what was going on in my community and the world. I used to read the Philadelphia Daily News, the Philadelphia Inquirer, and the Focus newspapers. I recalled that in the back of all these papers were advertisements for various things, including Help Wanted ads, which led to Human Resource departments linked to hiring managers.

Before I could move in the right direction, I had to really take stock and look at the environment. I revisited my analysis to make sure it was as reality-based as possible. It was for my advancement, so it only made sense to be 100% honest with myself.

Chapter Twenty-Three
Breaking into Business

"I've learned that fear limits you and your vision. It serves as blinders to what may be just a few steps down the road for you. The journey is valuable, but believing in your talents, your abilities, and your self-worth can empower you to walk down an even brighter path." ~ Soledad O'Brien

My analysis revealed external threats as well as opportunities to align work with my capabilities and many more strengths than I had weaknesses. Combined with my values, I considered the statistics associated with the trends affecting the economy and technological breakthroughs. To fully evaluate my strengths and weaknesses when faced with opportunities and threats, I sought out ways to emphasize my strengths and overcome my weaknesses. I got determined to do what was needed to provide my child with a safe and stable home life.

I knew I had to capitalize on opportunities for growth to minimize those threats. For instance, I focused on what was realistic and attainable in areas where I knew I could progress. I reflected on my vision of life. After analyzing who I was and where I came from, I was able to set clearer goals and objectives. These were my goals:

- Secure employment in a respectable business with timely opportunities for advancement where I can use my abilities and grow my skills.

- Become free of any association with the Department of Public Welfare and any other form of public assistance.
- Live in a safe place away from notorious drug-infested areas.

These were my objectives I set over four years to achieve goals:

By year-end 1990:

- Earn my General Equivalency Diploma (G.E.D.); meant I had the United States high school-level academic skills
- Find an entry-level business job through the classified ads in the Philadelphia Inquirer, Daily News, and Focus newspaper classified ads
- Save money and buy appropriate business attire
- Find reliable and reasonably priced childcare
- Secure employment in an office environment

By year-end 1991:

- Enroll in Community College of Philadelphia (CCP)
- Stabilize lodging via decent and affordable housing

By year-end 1994:

- Earn enough money to enroll my son in private school

I maintained a mental account, and even a few written notes, of all my plans. They would become the basis by which my thoughts and actions would continue flowing toward my desired future state.

I knew it would require a lot of mental work on my part to become the type of woman I wanted to be—the type who made a difference in this world. A woman like Eleanor Roosevelt, at the time, the longest-serving First Lady of the United States from 1933-1945.

I admired Mrs. Roosevelt tremendously. Not just because we were born on the same day, but because she accomplished so much in her efforts to bring about positive changes in our nation and to this world. She had become a voice for those economically disenfranchised during the Great Depression, mainly working women, African Americans, youth, and tenant farmers.

Following her 'husband's death during his fourth term, Mrs. Roosevelt was appointed by President Truman to the United Nations Commission on Human Rights. One of her most notable positions was as Chairperson of that organization. Her involvement led to the 1948 adoption of the Universal Declaration of Human Rights (UDHR), an international document that states basic rights and fundamental freedoms to which all human beings are entitled.

Now, I don't recall reading about Eleanor Roosevelt's accomplishments during my public-school education. If I had, who knows? I may have been inspired to hang in there with school a little longer. I had read in one of her published works that in 1913 she increased her managerial skills. That one change boosted her self-confidence and allowed her to become more independent. She possessed the will-power to change. I wanted to display that type of power and build my self-esteem. I was encouraged. I bought and read the city papers every chance I got.

I came across the Community Focus Newspaper, which was distributed by Print Media and considered the largest bilingual community newspaper in Pennsylvania. In that paper, I spotted an advertisement for free G.E.D. testing (limited time only). The exam was being administered at Community College of Philadelphia (CCP)—apparently, in an attempt to encourage those in the community to meet one of the college's enrollment eligibility requirements. I immediately called the phone number in the paper and scheduled myself for the exam.

On September 10, 1990, after anxiously trekking through public transportation to get to CCP, I signed in to sit for the exam. I was a little nervous because most people spent at least a couple of months studying and preparing to take the exam. Before the test started, I quickly imagined myself blending into the student body on the college campus after passing.

As I started to go through each part, it was apparent I was being tested on my ability to read and write and understand the standard written English in context as well as several areas within Social Studies, Science and Mathematical Reasoning. I focused all of my effort on providing the best answers and responses from what I could recollect in my prior years of schooling. I erased answers and second-guessed myself a few times. Once my pencil was placed onto the desk and my test booklet handed over to the test administrator, I got a great deal of satisfaction from taking another step in a positive direction. The unfounded feeling of nervousness I had when I entered the building was now a sense of empowerment.

During the next couple of weeks, while waiting for my test results, I continued to scan classified ads for entry-level jobs. I knew I had to get interview-ready. I checked out Payless Shoes, the Jaclyn Smith Powerful Women's collection at Kmart, and the Thrift Store on Kensington Avenue. I coordinated an impressively smart-looking, yet affordable, business attire ensemble in anticipation of being hired in the near-real future.

Taking a short break from job hunting, I went to the movies on September 19, 1990, to see Goodfellas. This movie both entertained and enlightened me. I especially took note of a statement by the main character, Henry Hill, who said, "For us to live any other way was nuts ... If we wanted something, we just took it. If anyone complained twice, they got hit so bad, believe me, they never complained again." Wow. What an exploitative way of thinking and living to excel through life.

This movie was based on a true-life story. Watching it solidified even more what I knew I had to do (spoiler alert if you've never seen Goodfellas). In the end, the main character, Henry, despised becoming part of the working class, which is what I yearned for daily. While I didn't want to be a schnook, doing shitty work in return for bum income, as Henry described himself in his new hidden identity, I figured earned bum income would be better than none. Bottom line, I wanted to catch a subway to work and earn a paycheck that would eventually help me break free from poverty.

The following week, I spotted a job listing within the help wanted ads in the Community Focus Newspaper for Prudential Insurance Company of America. I had no idea where Fort Washington, PA was before looking on a map, but once I did, I settled in my mind anything less than an hour away was doable. I called and inquired about the posted Receptionist or Secretary position. I was elated about having a confirmed interview date and time.

As the interview wound down, I was asked if I spoke Spanish. I confirmed I did and was asked if I would be interested in the opportunity to interview for a call center position. I hesitated until they mentioned it paid about $1 or more an hour, at which point I said, "Yes, 'I'm very interested!" They required me to interview in Spanish. During the interview, I spoke a bit of slang Spanish. I was concerned but realized it didn't matter when Yvette Rosendo, the hiring supervisor, instructed Human Resources to make me a job offer. I was so happy to be joining Yvette's team of customer service representatives who handled the American Association of Retired Persons (AARP) account in the Customer Communications Division.

I asked about future opportunities for advancement. Yvette informed me about positions in her department and others that included selling Prudential products if I passed exams and got licensed. It was clear becoming an insurance agent required in-depth knowledge of AARP-branded long-term care insurance and supplemental health products such as Prudential Medicare Supplement. The challenge served as the jolt that sparked the plug, which would ignite my passion to not only succeed in the role offered but other roles as well.

I asked about how hard it was to study and register for the Fellow, Life Management Institute (FLMI) professional development program that provided an industry-specific business education in the context of the insurance and financial services industry. It covered concepts intending to build a deeper understanding of the insurance business. Thoughts of what I could grow into turned into excited me and I wondered how my engine could repeatedly get upgraded over time, along with my income.

On September 28, 1990, I received my G.E.D. exam results. My heart nearly leaped out of my chest when I read the word: PASS. The icing on the cake was my writing score. Not only was it my highest score but it ranked 92 in the U.S. percentile! I felt invincible.

A couple of days later, I celebrated my son's first birthday with a party at McDonald's on 2nd and Lehigh Avenue. In my secret way, the party served as a celebration for me as well, for my G.E.D. accomplishment.

On Monday, October 8, 1990, three days away from my eighteenth birthday, I started my new job in Corporate America. During my forty-five-minute commute, I "kept hope alive" as I took a bus, subway, railway train and another bus from the train station in Fort Washington to Prudential's business office. I took in the view along the way, admiring the newly built and freshly painted single-family homes lining the streets. Some sported elegant brass lamps by their front doors, while most had well-manicured green lawns. It was refreshing to be surrounded by the never-ending array of brightly colored plants and roses planted in landscaped front gardens.

On my eighteenth birthday, I was in the mood for food from the restaurant located at 4535 N 5th Street. I would even have settled for the one closer to home at 3824 N 5th Street. Instead, I got to Wil's house after a long workday and traveling across county lines to find Nel looking tore up from the floor up. She hardly came around Hancock and Cambria, but she wanted to be there because her new boyfriend was selling drugs on that corner.

He had recently broken up with a girl nicknamed Cujo, and she was not taking it lightly that he had moved on to Nel. I asked Nel if she fought back because her face looked like someone beat it against the sidewalk. She said she didn't get a chance to do much, which was evident from the gigantic lumps on her face. Nel was not a bad person. She meant well. It was just always about her, and she spent her youth sheltered and treated like a princess, so she never had to learn to fight back.

Cujo knew Nel was a close childhood friend of mine, and when she got done with Nel, she told her she'd be looking for me when I got home from work. I couldn't take my work clothes off fast enough. I put on a t-shirt, sweat pants, and sneakers to prepare for what had become natural. I took off my fake pearl necklace set one piece at a time and slapped some Vaseline on my face before making my way to the corner of Hancock and Cambria. Cujo knew where to find me, but I had to get it over with since it was not if, but when, the fight occurred.

As soon as I arrived, neither one of us had any words. We ran up to each other and started punching and slapping the shit out of each other's faces with all our might. When I say, "with all our might," I'm not exaggerating because of all the fights I had ever been in, this girl made me work the hardest. The entire fight did not last long because we were both out of breath and on the ground in minutes. Cujo was short but thick. It took real effort to put her down, but when I finally did, and she realized my body was on top of her, she did one of the things she was infamous for and locked her teeth onto my right hand.

In that moment, I saw my aunt Santa and Wil nearby, and I yelled to them, "Unlock Cujo's jaws and get her teeth off my fingers!" Within seconds, her mouth was pried open, and my hand was set free. We both got up, dusted our bodies off, and took a few minutes to pull ourselves together. Neither one of us had more than a couple of minor scratches. As we stared each other down, there was an unspoken understanding the fight was over.

Someone grabbed me a White Mountain cooler, and I took it in one hand while hooking my son to my hip with the other. Leaving was not an option. I assumed the position on my aunt's side of the corner on Hancock and Cambria while Cujo took hers directly across from me. We both tried hard to look hard.

But, from that point on, we honored an unspoken agreement there was no need to continue the beef any further. Years later, we were around mutual friends. We talked to each other over a drink as if we never fought on my eighteenth birthday.

Chapter Twenty-Four
Breaking the Cycle

"Self-reliance is the only road to true freedom and being one's own person is its ultimate reward." ~ Patricia Sampson

The morning after fighting Cujo, I got up, put on a knee-length skirt, a matching blazer, a blouse, moderately comfortable pointy-toe heels, and went to work as if nothing happened. I didn't have any noticeable marks on my face, so I continued onward and upward. I was looking forward to breaking free from stupid street fights, corners filled with drug dealers, discarded drug paraphernalia, broken alcohol bottles, gunshots, police sirens, trash, and violence. North Philly was not a place for the faint of heart. If you didn't have any heart when you were born or moved there, you moved or got some pretty quick.

A few weeks later, I got a call about a fire at Wil's house. I panicked because my son was there during the day while I was working. When I arrived at my aunt's house on Hancock, my son was fine. I headed over to the house on Palethorpe Street where I saw the extent of the fire damage. The picture frames hanging on the walls were not completely ruined by the flames. I took a picture of my baby boy and me off the wall and attempted to take the print out of the frame, but the picture did not come out without tearing at the bottom and around the edges. I managed to get it out but part of it stuck to the glass. Evidence of the fire remained. Visible pieces of the burnt glass were now part of the picture itself.

Before departing with salvageable items, I spoke to a fireman. He said Wil's son lit a match in the basement trying to see in the dark, and when it burned his little finger, he dropped it, accidentally starting the fire. Then he said something I would never forget. He explained, "There are good fires and bad fires. The fire at this house was a good fire because no one was hurt."

When I returned to my aunt's house, Wil said she was going to move in with her mother's friend. My aunt then said my son and I could sleep in my cousin's old room since he wasn't living there at the time. The room was extremely small, and we both slept on the cold wood floor, huddled close together to provide each other warmth in the winter months. Those miserable nights prompted me to get serious about my saving habits. The only real debt I had left was the Watterson School of Business student loan.

I saved enough money to apply for a mortgage. When it was approved, the real estate agent told me how surprising it was to hear the bank was giving me a home loan when I didn't have a long-term employment record or any real credit. By the grace of God, on December 5, 1990, I signed a Corestates Mortgage Disclosure Statement for a property I put an offer on closer to Kensington. It was a small row home about a mile northeast from Hancock Street. I got $20,046 in financing on a thirty-year mortgage with the credit costing $36,977, at an interest rate of 8.75%. After 360 payments of $158, the total of what I borrowed, along with the cost of the loan would end up costing $57,024.

For the last time, I moved from the corner of North Hancock and West Cambria Streets to my own home located on the 3400 block of Hartville Street, Philadelphia, PA 19134. I tapped M.A.C. as we called the A.T.M. back then, paid the $25 mortgage recording fee and looked forward to my new future. I closed on my first house in March 1991. I got the keys, rushed over to the home and was greeted with giant white letters spray-painted on the front wall of the house directly across of the street. It read, "No, Spics!" I grabbed a

158

paintbrush and leftover paint I found in my basement and ran across the street to cover the racist remarks.

At work, we were required to answer phone calls by greeting AARP customers from all over the country with our first and last names. The person that wrote "No Spics!" across the street from my house must be related to the AARP member who called in on this particular day, I thought. Why? Because after greeting him, he angrily declared, "Lopez? Are you Mexican? I do not want to speak to any God damn Mexicans! I want to speak to an American!" Before I could say a single word, he said, "Get me an American, right now!" I thought about our training on not having to put up with abusive and rude callers. I wondered if this scenario met the criteria for my disconnecting. I recalled the lady in the Hamilton Mall who a couple of years earlier called me "Scum."

I wanted to give the AARP member a piece of my mind, which included a lesson in geography and history. I could have said, "Yo, don't get it twisted, fool! My parents were born in Puerto Rico, which is not in Mexico, and due to acts of imperialist politicians, regardless of where we are born, Puerto Ricans are 100% American citizens." But it didn't matter. Instead I imagined one day visiting PR when I could afford to venture onto the island for two weeks or more of exploring the cities, countryside, mountains, caves, and rain forests from end to end. To achieve this dream, I had to have a job which allowed me to save enough money.

Going back to school was no longer peripheral either and I enrolled in CCP. The Daily News featured an article on Bill Cosby speaking to students at Central High. They titled it, "Class Clown Fails to be Funny." The article reported, "... Cosby delivers meandering and nonsensical remarks. ('You may live in a lower economic area, but your mind is wealthy.') ". I didn't get the title of the article. And like Cosby, I went to Central High and dropped out, only to later obtain a G.E.D to secure a job in business.

At Prudential, amazing women like Yvette Rosendo treated me like I mattered. Some of the memorable ones also included Sharon Wright, Fay Barrett, Leyda Paesch, Ada Figueroa, and Linda Evans. They helped me become better, at my job and as a working-class woman. It was there I met good men like Lawrence Haliday and Jim Smith, who were also allies. All were well-respected women and people of diverse backgrounds who saw my potential. I was appreciative of kindness they extended, much like the way my middle school teacher (Dorothy Page) treated me when she taught me to believe in myself, something I had periodically forgotten. Each showed me that regardless of where I grew up, my appearance, and the opinions people had about my mother or me, I could do anything I set my mind to accomplish.

Because it did take a village while working full-time, I took action, continuously course-corrected and steadily placed one foot in front of the other. My mother sometimes stayed in the basement and I paid her $50 a week to watch my son while I worked. She said I was going to pay someone else so it might as well be her.

My primary motivation was to use work to advance my mission. As I took steps in a new direction, I could see the sun peeking over the horizon to someplace better like I had imagined for my son and me. I understood my job provided a means to break the cycle of poverty and I was grateful to earn a decent wage. The poverty guidelines for 1992 stated that the annual incomes for a family unit of 2 was $9,190. I made slightly more before I turned 20. It felt great to achieve objectives aligned with my goals. Because of this, I believe it is never too late to start over and write a new chapter in your life story. I discovered my ability to tap into the power of mindset and method to transition from the streets to Corporate America; from the corner to a cubicle.

SUPPORT

THANK YOU FOR READING - WILL YOU DO ME A SOLID[43]?

If you enjoyed this book or think it can benefit someone else, pay it forward and pass it on to another person. If someone you care about is struggling with breaking through the badlands of life or into the next level of their professional journey, consider sharing a copy. Whether you gift it to them from Amazon or share your purchase, it makes no difference to me, but it might make a difference in their life. It could assist them in bringing forth a sense of resolve, freedom, or newfound purpose.

You might change their life or show them a different way to view the world. You can keep this book moving and share your thoughts or questions in various ways. Any feedback sent to the author at amervis@amervis.com will be used to refine the content of future books. Reviews on Amazon and Goodreads also go a long way. Even a few words help, and reading honest, authentic reviews as well as getting feedback written by real readers, would mean a lot to the author as well as others.

If you'd like to get a free growth strategy workbook based on concepts from this book and receive updates on future initiatives, please sign up at amervis.com. Within the document, you will find actionable resources and tools to help you define what success looks like for you. Success defined in a specific and measurable way so you can align your actions, track progress, and reach your destination! This free workbook will help you whether you:

- Know what you want to do but aren't sure how to do it
- Have an idea of what you want to do, but need a bit of help
- Don't know what you want to do, and not sure how to start

As Viola Davis said, be willing to own your story and share it!

P.S. If you'd like to order discounted copies of this book for your school, organization, book club or group of friends, go to amervis.com/contact.

---

43 Favor

ABOUT THE AUTHOR

Amervis López Cobb, a girl from North Philly, left Philadelphia, PA in 2006 to pursue a dream of heading an Information Technology organization. After accomplishing this goal multiple times over at several publicly traded Las Vegas-based companies, in 2019, she resurrected another dream. One which required her to acknowledge her past self was a hero in her own story and took action to make sure her future self was positioned to help others become heroes in theirs. To awaken or reawaken to dream. To shed who she was so she could become who she was always been destined to be. An accomplished business executive, speaker, and author, Amervis is a true testament against the propagation of false stereotypes. When she is not writing, Amervis is inspiring others to succeed through the power of Mindset and Method. She is living proof of what can be achieved by continuously seeking and applying new knowledge and developing what she refers to as the MM factor.

Mindset + Method = Success

She currently resides in Las Vegas and can be found online at…

www.amervis.com
linkedin.com/in/amervis
facebook.com/amervis.lopez

Who can change the world? Anyone. Even an outcast girl with a little curl, a not so graceful twirl and a bit of ambition!